JESUS

THE POWERFUL SERVANT

TIM SPIVEY

HEARTSPRING PUBLISHING · JOPLIN, MISSOURI

Toll-free order line 800-289-3300
On the web at www.collegepress.com

The 3:16 Series (Colossians 3:16)
"Let the word of Christ dwell in you richly . . . ."

Cover design by Brett Lyerla
Interior design by Dan Rees

Library of Congress Cataloging-in-Publication Data

Spivey, Tim, 1975–
    Jesus, the powerful servant / by Tim Spivey.
            p. cm. — (3:16 series)
    ISBN 0-89900-945-X (softback)
  1. Bible. N.T. Mark—Textbooks.   I. Title.   II. Series.
    BS2586.S75 2006
    226.3'0071—dc22

                                                    2006008696

HEARTSPRING'S 3:16 SERIES

The Apostle Paul encouraged Christians in the first century and therefore us today to **"allow the Word of Christ to dwell in us richly"** (Colossians 3:16, *NIV*).

The 3:16 Series is based on this verse in Colossians. The series is designed primarily for small group study and interaction but will also prove fruitful for individual study. Each participant is encouraged to read the chapter before the group's meeting. The interaction questions are designed to be the focal point of your group's discussion time.

Psalm 119:11 says, *"I have hidden Your Word in my heart that I might not sin against You."* One noteworthy feature of this series is that each study includes a suggested memory verse (a short verse or two from the passage that is being studied). A sheet of these has been included at the back of the book for you to take these verses with you wherever you go and refer to them throughout your day.

The HeartSpring Publishing website will continually be updated with small group ideas and tips to further enhance your study of each New Testament book in the 3:16 series. Be sure to log on to www.heartspringpublishing.com (College Press) frequently!

**"Let the Word of Christ . . . have the run of the house.
Give it plenty of room in your lives."**
(Col. 3:16 *The Message*)

PREVIEWING OUR STUDY OF MARK

TIM SPIVEY

When I ask people which of the four gospels is their favorite, seldom does anyone name the gospel of Mark. This is unfortunate, but not surprising. Mark does not have the "red print" of Matthew, the parables of Luke, or the riveting metaphors of John. Mark is just Mark, and that's OK. He brings his own offerings to the table. They are urgency, conciseness, and a vision of Jesus that we would do well to preserve.

I am so pleased with the title that College Press picked for this volume: *Jesus, the Powerful Servant*. This title expresses succinctly Mark's view of Jesus. In Mark, Jesus is the unrecognized Messiah who suffers and dies for the sins of the world. He is also the one who has the power to cast out demons, interpret the law in fresh ways, and raise from the dead. For Mark, Jesus is *the* Powerful Servant.

"The beginning of the gospel about Jesus Christ, the Son of God" (Mark 1:1). What a way to start a story! Mark wants us to know right up front what he is up to. He is writing to report good news of a kind that the world has never known. It is the good news of Jesus Christ, the Son of God. Good news to whom? Good news to anyone who will listen.

Mark is the shortest of the four gospels and is written with an urgency that is second to none within the pages of Scripture. Repeatedly, he uses the Greek phrase, *kai euthus*, "And immediately," to describe what happens. For Mark, the story of Jesus moves fast. If the Gospel of Mark were a movie, most of the soundtrack would play tense, fast music. During the crucifixion, the soundtrack would change to the dirge of a requiem, and then, as Mark declares that Jesus is raised, the soundtrack would begin to resemble *Ode to Joy*, or something like it.

Mark very succinctly unfolds a great life before us—that of Jesus the Son of God—with urgency, and with a talent for description that tickles the imagination.

For those seeking meaningful and abundant life in a culture that is hostile toward true followers of Jesus, Mark has good news. The life of Jesus is not something we look back on with fond memories as we might look back on the life of Abraham Lincoln or Winston Churchill. Jesus is right here, right now. This is why Mark uses the historical present over 150 times in his Gospel. Jesus is not a past-tense Lord! He lives, he heals, he works, he casts out, he teaches, he empowers. To speak of Jesus in the past tense is inappropriate for Mark—the traveling mate of the apostle Peter whose words still stir the hearts of people who stand in need of good news. Praise God that Mark's good news has not expired! It is still good news right here, right now. The good news of Jesus *will always be* good news.

Things happen quickly in the Gospel of Mark. Therefore, we dare not take our eyes off the pages. Mark, likely written earliest of the four Gospels, is written to Roman Christians who are living in a culture that is hostile toward their faith in Jesus. By telling us the story of Jesus in the way that he does, Mark shows us that not only can Christianity survive in a midst of hostility and suffering. It can thrive! Christian faith is tailor-made for such times. This is good news—good news of Jesus, the Son of God.

The goal of this book is to help you and your group develop a clearer picture of Jesus as a model for power and servanthood, and to bring the immediacy and urgency of his life and message into your life today.

Chapter One: Even the Demons Obey Him (Mark 1:21-28)

Our study of Mark begins with this remarkable story in which a demon-possessed man is healed by Jesus in the synagogue. As everyone stands in wonder, it is obvious that Jesus is no ordinary teacher. He is different. Even the demons obey him. This story reminds us that Jesus is powerful enough to cleanse us of our deepest sins. Nothing is too powerful that it cannot be removed by the Word of Christ.

Chapter Two: True Values (Mark 2:23-3:6)

Sparks fly when Jesus heals a man on the Sabbath—what appears to be a clear violation of biblical law. In truth, Jesus is acting in complete harmony with God's law. He says, "The Sabbath was made for man, not man for the Sabbath. So the Son of Man is Lord even of the Sabbath" (2:27-28). Tradition is one of our richest sources of spiritual nourishment. It can also be a downfall when we adhere to it rather than the core gospel. Knowing the heart of Jesus helps us live according to

Previewing Our Study of Mark

the law of the Spirit of life in Christ that has set us free from the law of sin and death.

Chapter Three: The Unforgivable Sin (Mark 3:20-35)

As his family tries to make excuses for his words and behavior, Jesus warns the Teachers of the Law against committing the sin that will not be forgiven. This is a scary idea. We all immediately want to know what this sin is and if we have committed it. This question is dealt with in this chapter. According to Jesus, the unforgivable sin is blasphemy of the Holy Spirit. What is blasphemy of the Holy Spirit? In its proper context, blasphemy of the Holy Spirit is attributing God's actions to Satan. It is saying or believing that God's action is in fact evil. As we come to know Christ, we come to recognize the difference between the overtures of his Spirit and the overtures of evil.

Chapter Four: Soil Test (Mark 4:1-20)

The parables of Jesus in Mark 4 deal with questions concerning the growth of God's kingdom. In Mark 4:1-20, Jesus tells a story about four types of people (represented by soil in the parable). Each soil type bears fruit according to the fertility of the soil. Evangelism is a spiritual process, and this story calls us to focus our energies on cultivating responsive soil. Where? *In us.* Why? Because the more fertile the soil of our heart is, the more fruit we will bear. Gospel seed grows and multiplies only in fertile and healthy soil.

Chapter Five: Calming the Storm (Mark 4:35-41)

The apostles face a genuine crisis of faith when a storm at sea threatens their lives. They wake Jesus to ask him if he cares what is happening. Jesus' reaction to the disciples is one of gentle questioning. "Why are you so afraid? Do you still have no faith?" Jesus marvels at their fearfulness. One of the most common corroders of faith is the lie Satan sells us, "God does not care what happens to you." It is easy to feel as though Jesus doesn't care when the storms of life buffet us. Jesus would have us remember that real peace is not the absence of storms. *He* is our peace in the midst of storms.

Chapter Six: Faith That Rescues (Mark 5:21-43)

In chapter five, Mark weaves together two touching stories of healing to show us that Christ is the healer of all—rich and poor, male and female, old and young. Christ is the Great Healer because of his love and no other worldly standard. At the same time, Jesus is quick to commend the faith of both Jairus and the bleeding woman. In fact, in the

Previewing Our Study of Mark

case of the woman with bleeding, Jesus goes so far as to say, "your faith has made you well." Neither Jairus nor the woman with bleeding come to faith *after* they are healed. They have faith in Jesus' ability to heal before he does it. All of this woven together teaches us that at the same time Jesus' healing is available to all, faith plays an important part in the healing process.

Chapter Seven: I've Got Some Good News and I've Got Some Good News (Mark 8:27-38)

This chapter deals with the question: Who is Jesus? While affirming Peter's remarkable confession of faith—he is the Messiah—Jesus teaches that he must suffer, die, and rise. He will not establish his glory and might through a dazzling military campaign against Rome. He will establish God's reign through humility, suffering, and death! It seldom occurs to us that greatness can come through servanthood rather than might. Yet this is precisely what makes Jesus so unique. Jesus was not put to death by the religious leaders of his day *in spite of* being the Messiah, but *because* he was the Messiah! He was put to death because he was the anointed one of God, and that meant not earthly glory, but self-sacrificial servanthood. Jesus lived to die for others. This is our Christ. This is our Messiah.

Chapter Eight: It Is Good for Us to Be Here (Mark 9:2-19)

On the mount of Transfiguration Peter, James, and John are given a glorious vision of Jesus, Elijah, and Moses together. An awestruck Peter's desire to build a monument for each of the them summons God's voice from heaven declaring, "This is my beloved Son, whom I love. Listen to him!" Jesus is not one among other people or things that are worthy of worship. He alone is worthy of worship, and he alone is the source of our doctrine and practice. He alone is to be our heart's desire.

Chapter Nine: Help My Unbelief (Mark 9:14-29)

When a father is at the end of his faith that anyone or anything can heal his demon-possessed son, he cries out to Jesus. In doing so, he models real faith for us. Obviously, his faith isn't limitless. However, he prays with what faith he has and asks God to provide the faith he doesn't have. This is the essence of real faith. Real faith is humble enough to admit when it is wanting, and hopeful enough to trust that God can provide the faith that is needed. Faith is not a theory. Faith is not logic. Faith is not optimism. Faith is a journey in which we believe the power of God and demonstrate that belief by living in the power of God and demonstrating the gospel's power by how we live.

Previewing Our Study of Mark

Chapter Ten: Those Who Are Not against Us Are for Us (Mark 9:38-50)

Most disciples are confronted at one point or another of their spiritual journey with the issue of where to draw the lines. Most of us will wonder at some point, "Who's in? Who's out?" This was John's day to deal with this tough question. On this occasion, John tells an exorcist who is carrying out his ministry in Jesus' name to stop. Why? "Because he wasn't one of us" (9:38). Jesus rebukes John, telling him, "Those who are not against us are for us." The same is true today. Jesus stands beside us in the spiritual climate of our day and urges us toward unity with those who do his ministry in his name. The stirring of unity in the church is something that makes Satan tremble with fear, because a united church is something against which his gates cannot prevail. For too long, Satan's gates have stood strong as an anemic and underweight church knocked politely on its doors. But the time has come for the church to storm Hell's gates together. If we do, his gates don't have a chance.

Chapter Eleven: Cleansing the Temple (Mark 11:12-25)

The cursing of the fig tree and the cleansing of the Temple are two of Jesus' most frequently misunderstood actions. This is no surprise, for on their own, these two events are very difficult to understand. When read together, however, these two events explain each other. At their core, both the Temple cleansing and the cursing of the fig tree are about the same thing—being faithful all of the time. Not only in season, but out of season as well. Not only in the Temple, but out of the Temple. Not only in the church building, but between Sundays as well. We should not be put off by Jesus' anger, but rather inspired by it to become more like him.

Chapter Twelve: Becoming a "Crosstian" (Mark 15:25-34)

When Jesus is crucified he fulfills his calling. As he is crucified, he gives us our calling. The cross calls us not just to receive its benefits, but to receive it as a way of life. The cross is more than a monument or a symbol for Christianity. The cross is the daily mission of the Christian church. Jesus died to give us something to imitate. Jesus did die to redeem us from our sins. However, the cross is more than atonement for our sins. The cross is both where Jesus dies in our place *and* where he invites us to die with him. In the cross, he invites us to joyfully accept suffering and joyfully bear the injustices and the oppression and rebellion of our world. This is the present and coming kingdom of God.

Chapter Thirteen: Go and Tell (Mark 16:1-8, 14-18)

The resurrection of Christ is the most wonderful and glorious event in the history of the world. The normal reaction (or so we think) to such wonders is praise and amazement. However, Mark tells us Mary, Mary, and Salome have a different response. They are terrified. What should amaze them terrifies them. God's work often does this because our humanness limits our ability to see what God is up to. Other times his power is so awesome it actually scares us. God doesn't want us to be frightened by his power but to be stirred by it. The resurrection's power stirs us to speak boldly when we might otherwise cower. The resurrection of Jesus foreshadows our own. This is soul food for all who would come after Jesus. He is the resurrection and life. All who believe in him will live even in death. All who follow Jesus will never die. If we believe this, these words of Jesus, all of their promises are ours. Hallelujah!

TABLE OF CONTENTS

JESUS THE POWERFUL SERVANT

CHAPTER ONE

EVEN THE DEMONS OBEY HIM

MARK 1:21-28

As mentioned in the introduction, the Gospel of Mark moves very quickly. In only the first twenty verses, John the Baptist preaches of Jesus' arrival, Jesus is baptized, and twelve apostles are called.

In verse 21, Mark slows down to tell us about the dawn of Jesus' "public" ministry. I'm so glad he did!

> They went to Capernaum, and when the Sabbath came, Jesus went into the synagogue and began to teach. The people were amazed at his teaching, because he taught them as one who had authority, not as the teachers of the law. Just then a man in their synagogue who was possessed by an evil spirit cried out, "What do you want with us, Jesus of Nazareth? Have you come to destroy us? I know who you are—the Holy One of God!"
>
> "Be quiet!" said Jesus sternly. "Come out of him!" The evil spirit shook the man violently and came out of him with a shriek. The people were all so amazed that they asked each other, "What is this? A new teaching—and with authority! He even gives orders to evil spirits and they obey him." News about him spread quickly over the whole region of Galilee (Mark 1:21-28).

It is significant that in all four gospels, Jesus begins his public ministry in the synagogue or Temple (see Matt 4:17,27; Luke 4:14-15; John 2:13-22). When Jesus begins his public ministry in Mark, he is teaching in the synagogue and, through a miraculous exorcism in the midst of the assembly, shows that even the demons obey him (1:27).

What is most striking about this story is where the exorcism takes place.

13

Jesus isn't in the desert. He is in the synagogue! He isn't in Las Vegas. He is in the synagogue! He isn't in Sodom and Gomorrah. He is in the synagogue! What is a demon-possessed man doing in the synagogue? Demon-possessed people were not allowed in the synagogue. So, who let this guy in?

He doesn't appear to "slip past the guards." It doesn't appear that those around him have any knowledge of his condition until the holiness of Jesus and his teaching causes the evil within to cry out in fear and worship. As such, the best explanation for how this man got into the synagogue is that by all appearances, he looked fine. No one could tell that he was demon-possessed including himself. The demons inside of him want no part of Jesus, so it seems unlikely that he would have knowingly gone into a place where Jesus was present. He entered the synagogue with a condition unbeknownst to him or others.

Most of us are accustomed to experiencing evil in forms more subtle than demon possession like lust, anger, greed or dishonesty. Sin's work among God's people too often goes unnoticed and unspoken. Even today, churches are filled with people who sit in church looking and acting normal while sin has its way with them. Many of us have sat in a pew, singing, praying, and listening, while secret sin remains hushed or disguised. Like the demon-possessed man in our story, we look fine by all outward appearances. Inside, however, sin is decaying our souls.

> **Sin's work among God's people too often goes unnoticed and unspoken.**

This isn't what God wants for us or for his church. God wants us to walk with Jesus every day. Christianity is more than a one-time transaction between us and God that results in our salvation, it is a lifestyle that is focused on following Jesus every day.

When we are baptized, we both enjoy the victory of Jesus over our sin and embrace a new life lived out in imitation of Jesus. Salvation should be reflected in Christlike living. Listen to what Paul says in Romans 6:1-4: *"What shall we say, then? Shall we go on sinning so that grace may increase? By no means! We died to sin; how can we live in it any longer? Or don't you know that all of us who were baptized into Christ Jesus were baptized into his death? We were therefore buried with him through baptism into death in order that, just as Christ was raised from the dead through the glory of the Father, we too may live a new life."*

God wants to fill each of us so full of the Holy Spirit that there is no room for evil to move in. This is what abundant life in Jesus is all about. Satan doesn't leave you alone once you become a Christian, and the need to keep your feet firmly planted at the foot of the cross is constant. We do this in many ways. None is more important than making room for Jesus' teaching in our lives.

The Power of Jesus' Teaching

It is the presence and teaching of Jesus that convicts the demon inside the man in the synagogue. We must continue to drink deeply of the wellsprings of Jesus' life and teaching. This kind of nourishment will keep our lives focused on Christ and free from the evil's seduction. Hearing the teaching of Jesus as often as we can is marvelous medicine for the soul.

I cannot tell you how many times I have found this Scripture true: "For the word of God is living and active. Sharper than any double-edged sword, it penetrates even to dividing soul and spirit, joints and marrow; it judges the thoughts and attitudes of the heart" (Heb 4:12). Today as much as ever, Jesus' teaching calls the best and worst out of us. Jesus' teaching calls me to worship, as I am humbled to listen to the very words of God. I am humbled to hear him say, "I love you," and humbled to hear him say, "Follow me." When I hear Jesus speak, whatever wickedness that is in me trembles, and my love for him is kindled afresh. To put it simply, Jesus' teaching nourishes what is best in me and confronts what needs changing in me. This is oxygen for the spiritual life.

In Matthew 12, Jesus reminds us how important this is for a healthy life as he speaks of the need to continually nourish one's love for God. I love the way that Eugene Peterson paraphrases verses 43-45 in *The Message*:

> When a defiling evil spirit is expelled from someone, it drifts along through the desert looking for an oasis, some unsuspecting soul it can bedevil. When it doesn't find anyone, it says, "I'll go back to my old haunt." On return it finds the person spotlessly clean, but vacant. It then runs out and rounds up seven other spirits more evil than itself and they all move in, whooping it up. That person ends up far worse off than if he'd never gotten cleaned up in the first place.
>
> That's what this generation is like: You may think you have cleaned out the junk from your lives and gotten ready for God, but you weren't hospitable to my kingdom message, and now all the devils are moving back in.

Even the Demons Obey Him

Slow Down!

Nothing injures our spiritual lives more today than the pace of our living. I love attending sports events. It really doesn't matter what the sport is. Bring it on; it's all good! What never ceases to amaze me at each event is the number of empty seats down front. I find myself wondering, "How can someone with those seats not use them?" I drool as I stare at the empty seats near the floor from my perch at the crest of the arena. I pick two seats and imagine my wife and me sitting together screaming in harmony. Without fail at about the end of the second quarter a man and woman sashay in and flop down in those seats. He usually looks like Brad Pitt's lost cousin. She looks like Nicole Kidman's better-looking sister. After half-time, they watch about half of the third quarter before they yawn, get up, and leave. What an abomination! The only thing worse than not using seats that good is using them in that way—a way that suggests that you don't think you're missing much.

Christians have been given a great gift. In Christ, we have seen God up close and personal. We should treat the opportunity to walk with Jesus as priceless. We should not get there in the second quarter and leave in the third. We should get there early, enjoy every minute of it, and not let anything drag us away. The heart of discipleship is hospitable to the kingdom message.

If we want to keep our lives hospitable to Jesus' kingdom message, *we have to slow down*. Making our lives hospitable to God's kingdom message is the best way to continue to grow in Christ. We spend a lot of time in the fast lane. Prayer, worship, confession, repentance, fasting, and other spiritual disciplines can help us continue to grow after we become Christians. They can also keep evil far from us.

There Is Nothing He Can't Heal

Mark tells this story about a man who may or may not have even been aware how deeply evil had taken root inside of him. He does it because he wants us to witness the power of Christ for life change that is available to all of us. Jesus says to the demons, *"phimotheti kai exelthe ex autou."* The modern English equivalent is, "Shut up and come out of him." When Jesus speaks, the evil inside this man screams out in submission to the power of the authoritative teaching of Jesus Christ. It was true, and still is, "that the presence of the Savior is the torment of the devils."[1]

Most of us are willing to admit that from time to time—and maybe even right now, we have some bad habits that we just can't kick; some lifestyles we just can't get away from; some compulsive natures that we can't control. You might say, "It can't happen. I've tried so many times, and it has never worked. It isn't going to work today." That is Satan talking and he's scared. He knows who Jesus is . . . he knows that if Jesus tells him to leave, he must leave. If you will open yourself up to Jesus, the evil that has held you captive for so long can be healed. This doesn't necessarily mean you are demon-possessed. It may just mean that Satan has gotten a foothold in your life.

You may be thinking, "I can't do it." You're right. You can't. But Jesus can. Evil doesn't come out easily, but it comes out all the same. Why? Because even the demons obey him.

The good news is that the Jesus who drove out those unclean spirits long ago with an authoritative word is alive today, speaking such words to today's sin-bound people. His Word is powerful enough to cleanse any sin in your life. Let him declare to your unclean spirit, "Be silent, and come out." Let him say to the spirits of selfishness, jealousy, dissension, and envy, "Be silent and come out." Let him order any spirits of sorcery, idolatry, and witchcraft to "be silent and come out." Ask him to say to the spirits of sexual addiction, drunkenness, and rebellion, "Be silent and come out." To the spirits of doubt, fear, worry, and anxiety, let him command, "Be silent and come out." To the spirits of prejudice, hatred, and bigotry, the gospel says, "Be silent and come out." That's what he did for the demon-possessed man on that day. He can do it for you. As Mark says, "This is the beginning of the gospel about Jesus Christ, the Son of God." 1:16

---

[1]See Thomas C. Oden and Christopher A. Hall, eds., *Mark*, Ancient Christian Commentary on Scripture (Downers Grove, IL: InterVarsity, 1998) 21. Quote is attributed to Bede the Venerable, in *Homilies on the Gospels*. Bede's life is dated 673–735 AD.

Servants Like Jesus

1. What teaching of Jesus has made the strongest impact on your life?

2. What is the most amazing spiritual "turnaround" you've ever seen in a person's life? What made it possible?

3. Define the phrase, "Spiritual Warfare." Give some examples of spiritual warfare today.

4. Why do you think people go on sinning even after coming to Christ?

5. If you had sin in your life, to whom would you go for care?

6. Spend some time repenting of unconfessed sin and accept the forgiveness of Jesus.

> **Memory Verse**
> **Mark 1:26-27**
>
> *The evil spirit shook the man violently and came out of him with a shriek. The people were all so amazed that they asked each other, "What is this? A new teaching—and with authority! He even gives orders to evil spirits and they obey him."*

CHAPTER TWO

TRUE VALUES

MARK 2:23–3:6

I f you have ever sustained a cut that required stitches, you will know that doctors recommend you come back and have the stitches removed after about five days. If you don't, your body will begin to heal the stitches right into the fabric of the skin. Skin and stitches become one. This is the essence of what had happened over time with God's law and religious tradition. Tradition had been absorbed right into the law. Law and tradition had more or less become one to the religious leaders of Jesus' day.

One Sabbath Jesus was going through the grainfields, and as his disciples walked along, they began to pick some heads of grain. The Pharisees said to him, "Look, why are they doing what is unlawful on the Sabbath?" He answered, "Have you never read what David did when he and his companions were hungry and in need? In the days of Abiathar the high priest, he entered the house of God and ate the consecrated bread, which is lawful only for priests to eat. And he also gave some to his companions." Then he said to them, "The Sabbath was made for man, not man for the Sabbath. So the Son of Man is Lord even of the Sabbath." Another time he went into the synagogue, and a man with a shriveled hand was there. Some of them were looking for a reason to accuse Jesus, so they watched him closely to see if he would heal him on the Sabbath. Jesus said to the man with the shriveled hand, "Stand up in front of everyone." Then Jesus asked them, "Which is lawful on the Sabbath: to do good or to do evil, to save life or to kill?" But they remained silent. He looked around at them in anger and, deeply distressed at their stubborn hearts, said to the man, "Stretch out your hand." He stretched it out, and his hand was completely restored. Then the Pharisees went out and began to plot with the Herodians how they might kill Jesus (Mark 2:23–3:6).

At the end of Mark 2 and the beginning of chapter 3, Jesus finds himself crossways with the Pharisees who were arguably the most influential religious leaders among the Jews during Jesus' time. To say that he gets himself "crossways" is ironic given that they sit down and plot to kill him because of what happens in this story (3:6). Wow! What did he do? He did something that even today makes some people angry—*he tampered with tradition.* His opponents saw the situation differently, believing Jesus violated God's law itself! Over time the line between tradition and law blurred to the point that they were virtually indistinguishable to the Pharisees.

Understanding the Context

It was the Sabbath day; all work was forbidden and healing was considered "work." The Jewish law was definite and detailed about this. Medical attention could be given *only if a life was in danger.* For example: a woman in childbirth might be helped on the Sabbath. If a wall fell on anyone, enough material might be cleared away to see whether the person was dead or alive. If the person was alive, he might be helped; if the person was dead, the body must be left until the next day. A fracture could not be attended to and a cut finger might be bandaged with a plain bandage but not with ointment. At the most, an injury could be kept from getting worse, but it must not be made better.

All of this sounds a bit rigid to those of us living in the 21st century. However, to protect the Old Testament law, religious leaders over time began to "build fences" of tradition around it to ensure that it was honored in every way. Over time the line between God's actual commands and human commentary on those commands became increasingly blurred. Eventually, tradition became law as though God himself had spoken their editorial.

> Eventually, tradition became law.

By the time Jesus was born, the Pharisees had developed a system of 613 laws, 365 negative commands, and 248 positive laws. Many of these laws pertained to the Sabbath. The Sabbath was taken extremely seriously by all Jews and especially by devout Jews. A strict Jew might not even defend his life on the Sabbath. On one particular occasion during the Maccabean wars resistance broke out and some of the Jewish rebels took refuge in caves from Syrian pursuit. Josephus, the

Jewish historian, tells that although the Syrians gave them the chance to surrender, they refused. Instead, "they fought against them on the Sabbath day, and they burned them as they were in caves, without resistance and without so much as stopping up the entrances of the caves. They [refused] to defend themselves on that day because they were not willing to break in upon the honour they owed to the Sabbath, even in such distress; for our law requires that we rest on that day."

When Pompey, the Roman general, was besieging Jerusalem, the defenders took refuge in the Temple precincts. Pompey proceeded to build a mound from which he might attack them from above. He knew the beliefs of the Jews and he built on the Sabbath day. The Jews did not lift a hand to defend themselves or to hinder the building, although they knew that by their Sabbath inactivity their lives were doomed.

Despite their practice of compulsory military service, the Romans exempted the Jews from military service because no strict Jew would fight on the Sabbath. In general, the orthodox Jewish attitude toward the Sabbath was rigid and unbending. This is why the Pharisees were so outraged by Jesus' behavior on this occasion.

While few of us would argue that Jesus should be killed for causing a little trouble, it might seem to some that Jesus picked this fight. After all, did he really need to heal this guy on the Sabbath? Why not wait a day to do it instead of stirring up a hornet's nest? This man's life was not in danger; physically he would be no worse off if he were left until tomorrow. Moreover, why embarrass the Pharisees like that? From what we can tell in the text, they are simply sitting there minding their own business, yet Jesus seems to bait them intentionally.

Jesus tells the man with a withered hand to rise and stand where everyone can see him. Very likely Jesus wishes to make one last effort to waken sympathy for the stricken man by showing everyone his misery. More certainly, Jesus wishes to demonstrate this point in such a way that no one could possibly fail to see it. Jesus heals the man with a withered hand *very* publicly and immediately. Mark then informs us that this healing begins the plotting of Christ's crucifixion.

Understanding God's Will

It would be a mistake to take this story and jump to extreme conclusions. Too many simply assume, "The Sabbath is over, and we do not have to obey it. End of application." *Jesus is not saying that the Sabbath is irrelevant or passé.* On the contrary, Jesus obeys the Sabbath faithfully while he is on earth. Jesus never teaches, "Don't keep the Sabbath." He reveals God's true intent for Sabbath. The essence of

Sabbath is goodness, the restoration of life, and the worship of God. God created the Sabbath for his divine purposes—recuperation, healing, rest, and worship. Accordingly, Sabbath should not lead one to avoid all work to the extent of passing up the opportunity to give life.

Jesus asks the Pharisees, without provocation and in public view, "Is it better to do good on the Sabbath or to do evil?" In other words, "Is it the will of God that this man remain in suffering, or that I avoid work?" He is not choosing between right and wrong. Jesus is choosing what is *most* right.

To Jesus, not all law is created equal. This story is one among several others in the New Testament in which he declares the "weightier matters" of the law (cf. Matt 23:23). Healing a person on the Sabbath is not a violation of God's law. It is the fulfilment of it. As Jesus says, *"The Sabbath was made for man, not man for the Sabbath. So the Son of Man is Lord even of the Sabbath"* (Mark 2:27b-28).

In order to know the intent of the law, we must know the God who spoke the law. That is, we must get to know Jesus, the fulfilment of the law. Because Jesus is God, and because the Father is in the Son in complete harmony, and because Jesus was full of the Spirit of God, Jesus is able to speak with both authority and clarity regarding the intent and priority of these commands.

> In order to know the intent of the law, we must know the God who spoke the law.

The Pharisees had lost sight of the heart of law, and the heart of God that the law reflects. How does such a thing happen?

Robert C. Roberts once said, "There's something comfortable about reducing Christianity to a list of do's and don'ts, whether your list comes from mindless fundamentalism or mindless liberalism: you always know where you stand, and this helps reduce anxiety. Do's-and-don'ts-ism has the advantage that you don't need wisdom. You don't have to think subtly or make hard choices. You don't have to relate personally to a demanding and loving Lord."[1]

Authentic Christianity is lived in relationship with God. Knowing God is the first duty of each Christian. If loving God is not our first priority, we can expect our faith to grow as dry as old Saltine crackers or to go astray on account of either legalism or libertinism.

John Ortberg reflects:

> Conforming to boundary markers too often substitutes for authentic transformation. The church I grew up in had its boundary markers. A prideful or resentful pastor could have kept his job, but if ever the pastor was caught smoking a cigarette, he would've been fired. Not because anyone in the church actually thought smoking a worse sin

than pride or resentment, but because smoking defined who was in our subculture and who wasn't—it was a boundary marker.

As I was growing up, having a "quiet time" became a boundary marker, a measure of spiritual growth. If someone had asked me about my spiritual life, I would immediately think, 'Have I been having regular and lengthy quiet time?' My initial thought was not, 'Am I growing more loving toward God and toward people?'

Boundary markers change from culture to culture, but the dynamic remains the same. If people do not experience authentic transformation, then their faith will deteriorate into a search for the boundary markers that masquerade as evidence of a changed life.[2]

I believe that Ortberg's analysis of the modern-day church explains well what is going on in this story. The Pharisees had built fences around the law to protect it, and now those fences were hurting the broader cause of the law. For instance, in this case, their passion for Sabbath observance leads them to the murder of Jesus.

There are still those who strain gnats and swallow camels. There are still those who obey the Sabbath and neglect the weightier matters of law: justice, mercy, and faithfulness. These are people who forsake the unity of the body of Christ because a certain group does not "do church" the way they think they should. Some forsake the unity of the body because others do not agree with them on every jot and tittle of doctrine. Still others have built fences around Scripture to the point where tradition and Scripture itself have become virtually indistinguishable.

There is a great difference between knowing *about* God and knowing God. The Pharisees knew about God. They thought they knew the law, and they thought they kept the letter of the law. The Pharisees thought that they knew God's divine will, and yet, on this occasion, he stood face to face with them, and they did not recognize him. They were so blinded by their legalism that they could not see God. Jesus fulfilled the law by living it perfectly. He lived the law perfectly because

> There is a great difference between knowing *about* God and knowing God.

his unity with the Father was beyond measure. God is not particularly interested in cognitive knowledge of him apart from true knowledge of him. God is not a subject to be studied like mathematics or chemistry. He is a *person* who desires to know us and be known by us.

On a day like that one in the synagogue, or on a day like today in the church, knowing the heart of Jesus helps us live according to the law of the Spirit of life in Christ that has set us free from the law of sin and death. Therefore, we focus on the weightier matters of the kingdom like justice, mercy, and faithfulness. We seek first the kingdom, which is a kingdom of healing, that desires to bring all to an eternal Sabbath—where the redeemed will stand whole and unwithered in the presence of God ready to worship. [2:16]

_____

[1]Robert C. Roberts, in *The Reformed Journal* (Feb. 1987), *Christianity Today*, vol. 31, no. 9.
[2]John Ortberg, "True (and False) Transformation," *Leadership* (Summer 2002) 102.

24

✠

C
H
A
P
T
E
R

2 *True Values*

Servants Like Jesus

1. What role, if any, does Sabbath play in your life?

2. Think of a time when an ethical dilemma is created by having to choose between two "rights." How do we decide which "right" to choose?

3. How do we distinguish essential/core doctrine from matters of opinion or tradition?

4. What role does tradition play in the life of faith?

5. Is it possible to know God without knowing much about him?

6. Is it ever okay to "rock the boat"? Even if people get upset? Give some examples of holy "boat rocking."

Memory Verse Mark 2:27-28	*Then he said to them, "The Sabbath was made for man, not man for the Sabbath. So the Son of Man is Lord even of the Sabbath."*

CHAPTER THREE

THE UNFORGIVABLE SIN

MARK 3:20-35

It is a law of nature that all parents will embarrass their children. Though it will most likely happen far earlier, it is certain to happen during the teen years. Parents often say that it is payback for the embarrassment children cause them when they are younger. If you were to ask my mother for the time when I embarrassed her most, she would probably struggle to narrow the field.

The first time I actually gave money toward the work of the church was such an occasion. Though only four years old, I had been well prepared by my mother for this special moment. I received fifty cents per week for allowance (not bad in those days). I had been coached that ten cents of it was to be designated for giving to the church every week. That's right, I was going to be a double-tither!

That Sunday the moment of truth finally came. I waited all the way through the sermon and communion for the magic moment. The prayer for the offering finally concluded and the trays were handed off. I got my money out of my pocket, and as the tray came by, I proudly threw my money in there with plenty of pizzazz so that everyone could see that *I* was putting money in the plate. I hoped that the inferior Christians around me could learn from *my* example, for I was a *double-tither!*

It was about thirty seconds after I had so jubilantly put my money into the plate with such panache that I realized that in the heat of the moment I had put my entire allowance in the plate!

My face went pale, as my forehead moistened. I had just given away my whole allowance! How was I supposed to get by without any allowance?

I did the only thing that was appropriate. I got up from my seat, and sprinted after the tray and began taking money back out of the plate, yelling, "I gave too much! I gave too much!" My poor mother never forgot her shame.

Apparently even Jesus embarrassed his family. By the time we get to Mark 3:20, Jesus has made a spectacle of himself on numerous occasions. On this occasion, it seems that he has embarrassed his family to the point where they finally feel they need to contain him somehow.

By this time Jesus' popularity seems to have grown tremendously. A crowd has gathered to see what he might do next. Not the kind of crowd that gathers on 3rd Street Promenade in Santa Monica to see the 6-year-old boy play the violin with his feet. This crowd has gathered to see if he really teaches as they had heard. They are there because they don't want to miss a miracle. As it turns out, the crowd gathers just in time for another holy moment to occur.

> Then Jesus entered a house, and again a crowd gathered, so that he and his disciples were not even able to eat. When his family heard about this, they went to take charge of him, for they said, "He is out of his mind." And the teachers of the law who came down from Jerusalem said, "He is possessed by Beelzebub! By the prince of demons he is driving out demons." So Jesus called them and spoke to them in parables: "How can Satan drive out Satan? If a kingdom is divided against itself, that kingdom cannot stand. If a house is divided against itself, that house cannot stand. And if Satan opposes himself and is divided, he cannot stand; his end has come. In fact, no one can enter a strong man's house and carry off his possessions unless he first ties up the strong man. Then he can rob his house. I tell you the truth, all the sins and blasphemies of men will be forgiven them. But whoever blasphemes against the Holy Spirit will never be forgiven; he is guilty of an eternal sin." He said this because they were saying, "He has an evil spirit." Then Jesus' mother and brothers arrived. Standing outside, they sent someone in to call him. A crowd was sitting around him, and they told him, "Your mother and brothers are outside looking for you." "Who are my mother and my brothers?" he asked. Then he looked at those seated in a circle around him and said, "Here are my mother and my brothers! Whoever does God's will is my brother and sister and mother" (Mark 3:20-35).

Jesus' family thinks he is out of his mind. The Scribes think he is evil. Yet, none of them can deny what he is doing. Their question is, how is he doing it? His family provides the insanity defense. The Scribes do what many people do when they witness something they have not seen before and do not know how to describe it . . . *they say it is evil.* "He does this by Beelzebub!" they say.

Jesus rebuts brilliantly both accusations with a simple illustration. He points out that casting out demons by the power of Satan does not make any sense. Why would Satan empower Jesus to tear down his kingdom? Good question.

In truth, the Scribes are half right. Jesus is destroying Satan's kingdom, but he is doing so by the power of the Holy Spirit, not by Beelzebub—the prince of demons. In Mark 3:26 Jesus makes his point clear, *"In fact, no one can enter a strong man's house and carry off his possessions unless he first ties up the strong man. Then he can rob his house."* Jesus implies that it is he who has tied up Satan, and that he is now in the process of plundering Satan's house.

Jesus then issues a stern warning to the teachers of the law, saying that they are in danger of committing the "unforgivable" sin. Immediately, we want to know what it is, and if we have committed it. We also wonder, "Is it really unforgivable?"

Is the unforgivable sin really unforgiveable?

Recognizing the Spirit's Work

According to Jesus, the unforgivable sin is blasphemy of the Holy Spirit. What is blasphemy of the Holy Spirit? In its proper context, blasphemy of the Holy Spirit is attributing something that God does to Satan. It is saying or believing that God's action is in fact evil.

In a broader sense, this story deals with spiritual blindness—particularly that of the teachers of the law. It is spiritual blindness that keeps them from seeing the Messiah for who he is.

If you have ever looked for your glasses even as they sit perched on top of your head or looked for the remote control while it is already in your hand, you have experienced in the physical realm the kind of blindness that the teachers of the law suffered in the spiritual realm. The kingdom of God has indeed come near, but they can't see it. So, they keep looking for the Messiah even as they behold him performing miracles before their eyes. They can't deny that something supernatural is taking place; they simply deny that it is coming from God.

This still happens. There are people who look at a church that is growing and vibrant and assume that what is happening is occurring because someone is "capitulating to the culture." In other cases, people might look at a friend who is head-over-heels in love with Jesus and quietly resent the passion of his or her spirituality. They think or say, "I bet they are just doing that to be seen," or, "That isn't genuine."

These sentiments carry within them the spirit of the scribes in Mark 3. Obviously, making a mistake does not damn a person. That is not what Jesus is getting at. Jesus is saying that a person who attributes what is of God to Satan is *in danger of* blaspheming the Holy Spirit.

Evil is real and should be watched for. However, we must avoid developing a scribal state of heart that can only see evil. Such a heart will only see good through a veil of suspicion, if it can see good at all.

Beholding the Glory of Jesus

We must come to know Christ well enough to recognize the difference between the overtures of his Spirit and the overtures of evil. As we grow in our walk with God, we learn to discern what is of him and what is not.

If Satan is being defeated, if people are coming to Christ, if they are renouncing their old lives, if they are embracing reconciliation and pursuing the heart of God, it is not by the power of Satan. Satan will not work against himself. Judge the tree by the fruit. If the fruit is good, be cautious about attributing it to the work of Satan. Instead rejoice, knowing that what you are witnessing is happening because of the binding of the strong man Satan by the Stronger One Jesus Christ.

Jesus says that we will know his work when we see it. When John the Baptist sends a delegation to Jesus to ask, "Are you the Messiah or should we wait for someone else?" Jesus never says, "Yes," but he answers through a simple recitation of what he is doing. He says in so many words, "Judge me by my fruit."

> Jesus told them, "Go back to John and tell him about what you have heard and seen—the blind see, the lame walk, the lepers are cured, the deaf hear, the dead are raised to life, and the Good News is being preached to the poor. And tell him: 'God blesses those who are not offended by me'" (Matt 11:4-6).

Today, many people who do God-honoring things are still accused of doing evil. Be assured that if you are doing good, people will criticize you. Why? Because every Christlike word, deed, attitude, and conviction plunders Satan's house. In his anger and desperation, the Evil One will lash out, drafting soldiers into his army in an attempt to halt the work of the Stronger One, Jesus Christ.

This will not work. Ultimately, Christ has

> Be assured that if you are doing good, people will criticize you.

gained the victory through his life, death, and resurrection from the grave. The strong man has been tied up, and his house has been plundered and will continue to be plundered by those who belong to the Stronger One, Jesus Christ.

The Joy of Plundering

As we join Jesus in his mission, we should note that his mission is one played primarily on *offense, not defense.* Jesus views himself as binder and plunderer. Jesus, the Stronger One, has bound the strong man, and stands at the front door of the house inviting the people of God to redeem those whom Satan has held captive as his treasures for too long. As his followers, we participate in this ministry.

Jesus' mission is played primarily on offense, not defense.

When a church reaches people with the gospel, Satan's house is plundered; when someone finds the courage to broach the subject of faith with a non-Christian friend after many years of having not done so, Satan's house is plundered. When the couple that was ready to divorce decides to recommit their marriage to God, Satan's house is plundered.

This story calls us to mission by reminding us that in Christ, the strong one Satan has been bound, and with Jesus Christ going on before, we enjoy the plundering of Satan's house of destruction and wickedness. We go on with our brother Jesus Christ, and we do battle as soldiers of the kingdom of God. We battle because we who were once slaves in Satan's house have been set free by the Stronger One, the Lord Jesus Christ. Hallelujah! 3:16

Servants Like Jesus

1. Can you think of a time when Jesus embarrassed you?

2. Why do we sometimes fail to recognize God's work when we see it?

3. Does the analogy that Jesus uses of his binding Satan and robbing Satan's house shock you?

4. Tell of a time when you saw Satan's house plundered.

5. What is the unforgivable sin . . . specifically?

6. Have you joined Jesus in his mission?

 Then he looked at those seated in a circle around him and said, "Here are my mother and my brothers! Whoever does God's will is my brother and sister and mother."

CHAPTER FOUR

SOIL TEST

MARK 4:1-20

Let me tell you about four people I know (names have been changed).

Michael was Jewish by birth and secular in faith. We pledged the fraternity together. We were roommates for the last two years of college. There were a few awkward moments when religion came up, but for the most part he treated my faith as though it were a hobby of mine. He respected my convictions. He would even come to hear me preach from time to time. His attitude toward it, however, was similar to that of a friend watching another friend's piano recital. For him, it was simply a hobby of mine, and he thought it was great to see someone so dedicated to what he loved.

God only knows how many thousands of hours we spent together. Over some of those hours we discussed faith issues. Ten years have passed since we first met and he doesn't seem a single inch closer to becoming a Christian than he was on the day that I met him.

And then, there was Patrick. He was converted in college. From that moment on, he seemed so strong in the faith. So strong, that he eventually became a church intern—and a good one at that. He had a great way with people. He was uncanny at sensing when the door was open to talk about matters of faith.

We were all so proud when he received admission and a fellowship to Stanford Medical School. He and I left school together ready to make an impact in our respective fields. Unfortunately today, only one of us is still a Christian. Patrick's faith seemed to dissolve as medical school and the lure of making money replaced God as the center of his life. Today Patrick isn't a practicing Christian at all. There are many who are still trying to get him to recover a lost interest. But in Patrick's mind Christianity is for the immature. To him Christians resemble a mother who wants her son to continue to play with his toy cars despite the fact that he's 40. Christianity was helpful to him in the past, but he feels that he needs to move on to things that are more here-and-now.

Kristin was a preacher's kid. I remember hearing her dad preach once when I was in high-school. He seemed like a really solid man of God. When we got word that she was coming to Pepperdine, we just knew she would be a solid addition to campus ministry and could have a tremendous impact on the campus. For a while, she did. She took the campus by storm spiritually during her freshmen year.

The problem is that college lasts four years and by the time her sophomore year was halfway through, we could see that her faith was in trouble. We tried to help in every way we could. I can remember the entire group of church interns (16 of them) praying for her.

At the end of her sophomore year, Kristin flunked out of school. And from there Satan seemed to have his way with her. She got pregnant out of wedlock twice, by different guys, moved out on her own to northern California, and hasn't been back to church since.

Thank God for Lee. He was such a tremendously spiritual young man. God had gifted him uniquely in his ability to relate to people. He was the Ferris Bueller of the campus. Lee gained tremendous spiritual influence within groups that had been off-limits to campus ministry for years. It was rare that a student would ever baptize another student. I'll bet he baptized a dozen.

Lee graduated and ended up going into youth ministry. After several years of influencing young people for Christ, he married and left to become a missionary in Africa, where he bears fruit to this day.

When I read the parable of the soils, I can't help but think of Michael, Patrick, Kristin, and Lee.

Again Jesus began to teach by the lake. The crowd that gathered around him was so large that he got into a boat and sat in it out on the lake, while all the people were along the shore at the water's edge. He taught them many things by parables, and in his teaching said: "Listen! A farmer went out to sow his seed. As he was scattering the seed, some fell along the path, and the birds came and ate it up. Some fell on rocky places, where it did not have much soil. It sprang up quickly, because the soil was shallow. But when the sun came up, the plants were scorched, and they withered because they had no root. Other seed fell among thorns, which grew up and choked the plants, so that they did not bear grain. Still other seed fell on good soil. It came up, grew and produced a crop, multiplying thirty, sixty, or even a hundred times." Then Jesus said, "He who has ears to hear, let him hear." When he was alone, the Twelve and the others around him asked him about the parables. He told them, "The secret of the kingdom of God has been given to you. But to those on the outside everything is said in parables so that, 'they may be ever seeing but never perceiving, and ever hearing but never understanding; otherwise they might turn and be forgiven!'" Then Jesus said to them, "Don't you understand this parable? How then will you understand any parable? The farmer sows the word. Some people are like seed along the path, where the word is sown. As soon as they hear it, Satan comes and takes away the word that was sown in them. Others, like seed sown on rocky places, hear the word and at once receive it with joy. But since they have no root, they last only a short time. When trouble or persecution comes because of the word, they quickly fall away. Still others, like seed sown among thorns, hear the word; but the worries of this life, the deceitfulness of wealth and the desires for other things come in and choke the word, making it unfruitful. Others, like seed sown on good soil, hear the word, accept it, and produce a crop— thirty, sixty or even a hundred times what was sown" (Mark 4:1-20).

There is a clear escalatory movement in the text from the soil in which the seed never can take root at all to the soil in which the seed takes root and bears tremendous fruit. That type of movement in the text suggests that *the focal point of the story is the last type of soil.*

The parables that Jesus tells for the rest of Mark 4 underscore the fact that he is concerned with the dynamics of kingdom impact. He talks about hiding a lamp under a bushel, and the kingdom of God being like a mustard seed that starts small and then grows to be enormous. In the parable of the soils, Jesus speaks to all who will listen about purpose and potential for kingdom impact.

> Jesus is concerned with the dynamics of kingdom impact.

Praise be to God that he does not force himself into relationship with people. Instead he chooses to love and to open the door to relationship with people. This doesn't mean that he is hands-off. Every day and every minute, God is scattering the seed of the gospel across the earth in various ways.

Some of the seed, like Michael, never takes root. It just never takes root. The gospel seed falls on the hard path. Seed was scattered in Michael's life, but Satan came and took it away because it had no root. Other seed will take root for a while, as in the life of Kristin. Eventually though, it is scorched by the sunny heat of life. When faith became too costly to her flesh, she left the faith. The gospel's roots in her were shallow. And so, today, despite her upbringing, she is far from God. God continues to throw gospel seed on her heart's soil in hopes it will someday take root. Then there are others like Patrick who, to put it in the words of Jesus, "like seed sown among thorns, hear the word; but the worries of this life, the deceitfulness of wealth and the desires for other things come in and choke the word, making it unfruitful." We all have seen this happen to people. Even committed disciples can feel the tug of wealth on the heart. This often happens to veteran Christians that have never really experienced the depth and riches of true relationship with God. Perhaps wealth, lust, or selfishness has kept you from bearing or experiencing the fruit that God wants to bear in your life. Others, like Lee, bear fruit that is 30, 60, or one hundred times what was sown. The gospel has taken root and is multiplying in miraculous ways.

It is my conviction that most of today's churches are comprised of soil types 2, 3, and 4. There are some in most churches that have little if any faith left and attend church out of habit or guilt. There are others who have more faith, but it is an impotent faith. It bears no fruit; it contains little joy or vibrancy. There are others—we'll put them among soil type 4—who are loving God with heart, mind, soul, and strength and loving their neighbors as themselves.

Without sounding overly cynical about the state of the contemporary church, I would suggest that soil type 4, that Lee type of fruit-bearing soil that Christ exalts in his story, is not the majority. Herein lies the problem of contemporary Christianity. Christian lives and churches are not making nearly the impact that they are capable of because the gospel hasn't fully taken root.

In the parable, the gospel does not fail to take root because the seed is bad. The problem isn't a seed shortage, or that seed hasn't been scattered on the soil yet. Rather, the soil is the issue. The problem is that some soil is better for planting than others.

In our efforts to do evangelism, we have often gone about it in a way that suggests scarcity of seed. "We need to spread the gospel." "There are people out there who have never heard the gospel." Of course this is all true. However, you never get the sense that a lack of seed—a lack of information—is the issue in this parable. Rather, it is a lack of fertile soil.

> The problem is not a lack of seed but a lack of fertile soil.

There were many who witnessed the acts of Christ who never believed. Coincidentally, they were religious leaders. There were others who followed for a while, and when the teachings got tough, they "turned back and no longer followed him" (John 6:66). Others followed a long time but never bore much fruit. There were still others, like Peter, James, and John, who bore great fruit.

Everyone heard the same teaching, often in the same doses, but not all responded in the same way. If the spreading of the gospel were the only factor in evangelism, everyone who heard would believe. But, we all know that isn't true. And if sheer effort on the part of the soil were all that were involved, then everyone that ever believed would be faithful to this day and have born 30-, 60-, or 100-fold fruit. This isn't the case either. There is more to the spreading of the gospel than either hearing or effort.

The Spiritual Process of Evangelism

Evangelism is a spiritual process. Perhaps we should focus our energies on cultivating responsive soil. Where? *In us.* Why? Because, in this parable, God is the one throwing around gospel seed. And, the more fertile the soil of our heart is, the more fruit we will bear.

The most important step in becoming an evangelist is becoming evangelized. Becoming a Christian entails more than cognitive assent to a set of facts about God. Conversion leads to the continual cultivation of our spiritual soil so that gospel seed will take root and grow in us. As it grows, you will produce a spiritual bounty.

Gospel seed grows and multiplies in fertile and healthy soil. This is why the only type of people you see involved in the conversion of others in Scripture are either new converts or apostles. Why? They are fertile soil. Churches that are going to produce a bountiful harvest are those whose ground is fertile. They are the churches in which the gospel has taken root and grows in strength and power. Fruit-bearing churches are always committed to worship and spirituality. God is at the center of everything we are and everything we do. Keeping him at the center of the church's mission keeps the soil of our hearts fertile.

> **Fruit-bearing churches are always committed to worship and spirituality.**

Churches that do not prepare the soil properly for the sowing of the gospel will be rendered fruitless by Satan or their own rootlessness. Or, to put it in the words of Jesus, "When trouble or persecution comes because of the word, they quickly fall away. Still others, like seed sown among thorns, hear the word; but the worries of this life, the deceitfulness of wealth and the desires for other things come in and choke the word, making it unfruitful."

We have a challenge. There are 195 million unchurched people in the United States, making the U.S. the third largest mission field in the English-speaking world and the fifth largest globally. How can we reach these people for Christ? Till the soil. Not just theirs. Ours.

I'm not sure we believe enough in the impact God can make through just one human life. Jesus tries to give us a glimpse. God is scattering gospel seed everywhere. If his seed falls on fertile soil, *it will take root*. Lives will change. People will give their lives to Jesus. The gospel will take root in them and they too will bear fruit—30, 60, and a hundred times over. 3:16

Servants Like Jesus

1. Which kind of soil does your heart represent?

2. Why is the gospel welcomed in some places and not in others?

3. What may be holding back the potential for fruitfulness in your life?

4. Make a list of people closest to you who are not Christians? How can you join God in tilling the soil of their hearts?

5. How do we prepare the soil of our hearts for the planting of gospel seed?

6. Spend some time in prayer asking God to make the soil of your heart fertile.

Again he said, "What shall we say the kingdom of God is like, or what parable shall we use to describe it? It is like a mustard seed, which is the smallest seed you plant in the ground. Yet when planted, it grows and becomes the largest of all garden plants, with such big branches that the birds of the air can perch in its shade."

CHAPTER FIVE

CALMING THE STORM

MARK 4:35-41

That day when evening came, he said to his disciples, "Let us go over to the other side." Leaving the crowd behind, they took him along, just as he was, in the boat. There were also other boats with him. A furious squall came up, and the waves broke over the boat, so that it was nearly swamped. Jesus was in the stern, sleeping on a cushion. The disciples woke him and said to him, "Teacher, don't you care if we drown?" He got up, rebuked the wind and said to the waves, "Quiet! Be still!" Then the wind died down and it was completely calm. He said to his disciples, "Why are you so afraid? Do you still have no faith?" They were terrified and asked each other, "Who is this? Even the wind and the waves obey him!" (Mark 4:35-41).

I love the show on the Weather Channel called, "Storm Stories." It's a documentary show that chronicles great natural disasters and talks about how tornados, hurricanes, and tsunamis work. The footage of the storms they show is absolutely incredible. It's one thing to watch the show and be filled with awe. It's something else to be involved in a great storm yourself. Rather than being entertained, you are terrified.

I used to love watching documentaries on the great earthquakes of history. And then, it happened. The day was January 17, 1994. At 4:31am, a 6.7 magnitude earthquake struck Northridge, California. In fifteen seconds, the most costly disaster in the history of the United States up to that time occurred. Fifty-one people died, and over 9,000 were injured. Portions of 11 major roads and 5 freeways leading into

Los Angeles had to be at least partially closed. In today's dollars, nearly $900 billion of property had to be replaced. I happened to be driving a car about 15 miles from the epicenter of the earthquake when it struck. People have asked me what it was like. It most closely resembles having the person riding shotgun in the car reach over and jerk the wheel back and forth as hard as they can while the person sitting behind you in the car grabs you by the shoulders and shakes you as hard as they can. Lots of fun.

The numerous and brilliant seismologists at Caltech discovered that the direct cause was a previously unknown fault nine miles beneath Northridge, a town in the San Fernando Valley. It was a "blind" fault, one that doesn't break the surface and make itself visible.

Blind faults, faults that lie beneath the surface unseen and cause problems suddenly, occur in life as well. No doubt, the disciples—and particularly the fishermen among them—knew the sea of Galilee's moodiness. In fact, the Sea of Galilee is positioned in a valley, and as such, is uniquely susceptible to quick weather changes and harsh storms. Just as people who live in southern California know that earthquakes can happen, the disciples knew that storms happen on the Sea of Galilee. Nevertheless, they didn't know *when* a storm might strike. Mark alone notes the fact that there were other boats out on the sea as well. This means the storm undoubtedly sneaked up on everyone who was at sea.

Does Jesus Care?

As the waves crash into the boat, the disciples go down and wake Jesus. What they exclaim is interesting, and it draws Jesus' ire. "Don't you care that we are all going to die?" they ask. Have you ever experienced that feeling? Something really bad happens and you begin to wonder if Jesus cares that something horrible is happening to you. A husband leaves, a child rebels, a job is lost, debt begins to suffocate joy in the house, and we want to know if somewhere along the line God stopped caring about us. Sometimes something bad goes on for so long that you can't help but wonder if either God has fallen asleep at the wheel of the universe, he doesn't like you, or he likes picking on you. These feelings are common but dangerous.

One of the most common corroders of faith is the lie Satan sells us, "God does not care what happens to you. He's got more important things to worry about. Do you think he cares what happens to you after what you did last weekend?" On and on he goes. We all know how much it impacts human relationships when we feel as though someone does not care about us. Our relationship to God is no different. If we come to believe that God doesn't care what happens to us, our love for God will be put under enormous strain.

The truth is that God always cares what is going on in our lives. The Bible tells us that even the hairs on our heads are numbered (Matt 10:30). We often think wrongly that love always seeks to halt any struggling of the loved at all costs. That is, if you love me, you won't let me suffer. This notion of love is foreign to Scripture. God's love for us is perfect and its ultimate expression came through his own suffering on the cross.

For us to equate love with a lack of suffering is to equate love with novocaine. Love is far deeper and more complex than that. In fact, sometimes love even causes suffering for the good of the loved or for the good of the relationship. At the very least, love sometimes allows the suffering of someone for their greater good. Something like this is taking place on the boat on this occasion I believe. God does not do away with all storms. That would not be true love. Love is found to be true when it is tested in the crucible of things like storms. That is also how faith is matured.

The most frequent command in all of Scripture is, "Do not fear." Why? Because fear articulates two things. **First**, it displays a lack of faith in God's care. **Second**, it shows that we believe that God is not in control.

The presence of Jesus means the presence of peace in the life of the believer. The presence of Jesus does not mean the absence of storms. The presence of Jesus means that Christ's calming presence and voice is there to still the tempests of life that threaten to sink us.

Jesus' reaction to the disciples is one of gentle questioning. "Why are you so afraid? Do you still have no faith?" Jesus marvels at their fearfulness. He asks them, "How can you still doubt?" They had watched him do so many amazing things and show such care for those in distress in the course of their time with him. Nevertheless, they lack the faith that Jesus can do anything about their situation. Their fear had grown greater than their faith.

Fear is kryptonite for Christian boldness. It has a paralyzing influence on people and churches. In the personal realm, it leads to insecurity and anxiety that God doesn't want for us. In the church realm a fearful, scarcity mentality causes churches to focus on the appeasement and preservation of its members rather than on the mission to which God has called them.

Fear is kryptonite for Christian boldness.

God's Word is a record of God's activity throughout history. Based on who he is and what he has done (especially in Christ), he wants us to trust in him. Trusting God sets us free from a life of anxiety that leads to emotional and spiritual paralysis. I understand this is easier said than done. However, he who is in us is greater than he who is in the world. God has not left us to fend for ourselves in the battle to rid our lives of fear. "God did not give us a spirit of timidity, but a spirit of power, of love and of self-discipline" (2 Tim 1:7).

> **Living in faith keeps us from being paralyzed by fear.**

The more we trust Jesus the more sleep we'll get and the less worrying we will do. Living in faith keeps us from being paralyzed by fear. Because of fear, many people live in a constant state of anxiety. That isn't the way God desires for us to live.

A freshman at Eagle Rock Junior High won first prize at the greater Idaho Falls Science Fair, April 26, 1997. He was attempting to show how conditioned we have become to alarmists practicing junk science and spreading fear of everything in our environment. In his project he urged people to sign a petition demanding strict control or total elimination of the chemical "dihydrogen monoxide."

And for plenty of good reasons, since it:

- Can cause excessive sweating and vomiting.
- It is a major component in acid rain.
- It can cause severe burns in its gaseous state.
- Accidental inhalation can kill you.
- It decreases effectiveness of automobile brakes.
- It has been found in tumors of terminal cancer patients.

He asked 50 people if they supported a ban of the chemical. Forty-three said yes, six were undecided, and only one knew that the chemical was H_2O (water). The title of his prize winning project was, "How Gullible Are We?" He feels the conclusion is obvious (source unknown).

Jesus views the apostles' anxiety in the face of the storm as a lack of faith. That means that, according to God's Word, the level of fear in one's life is a gauge of one's faith. Fear, or a lack thereof, functions as a faithometer. This does not mean God wants us to be apathetic, emotionally numb, or blind to danger or suffering. God wants us to trust more in his care and deliverance than we fear the tumults of this life.

With a few words, Jesus silences the very thing that seemed insurmountable to the disciples. The fact that Jesus is sleeping through the entire episode and has to be awakened should show us something about the calmness with which Jesus faced adversity. Jesus was peaceful because he knew the power of God. That is the kind of peace that God wants for us.

> Jesus was peaceful because he knew the power of God.

Christ's peace is something that is beyond our understanding. Paul speaks of it in Philippians 4:6-7:

> Do not be anxious about anything, but in everything, by prayer and petition, with thanksgiving, present your requests to God. And the peace of God, which transcends all understanding, will guard your hearts and your minds in Christ Jesus.

Just as stark as the contrast between the reaction of the disciples and Jesus to the storm is the contrast between the fearful and the faithful today.

The fearful person moans. The faithful person sings.

The fearful person sulks. The faithful person dances.

The fearful person trembles in fear of law. The faithful person trusts in the grace of Christ.

The fearful person cowers. The faithful person preaches.

The fearful person cries out in doubt. The faithful person awakens Christ in confidence.

The fearful person denies Christ. The faithful person will die for Christ.

The fearful person accomplishes little. The faithful person moves mountains.

The beautiful truth is that the same Christ who slept during the storm and awoke to calm it with merely a few words from his mouth, lives in us. And so, we should live fearlessly. Why? **Because we have Christ sleeping within us.**

Augustine once said:

> When you have to listen to abuse, that means you are being buffeted by the wind. When your anger is roused, you are being tossed by the waves. So when the winds blow and the waves mount high, the boat is in danger, your heart is imperiled, your heart is taking a battering. On hearing yourself insulted, you long to retaliate; but the joy of revenge brings with it another kind of misfortune—shipwreck. Why is this? Because Christ is asleep in you. What do I mean? I mean you have forgotten his presence. Rouse him, remember him, let him keep watch within you, pay heed to him. . . . A temptation arises: it is the wind. This is the moment to awaken Christ and let him remind you of those words: "Who can this be? Even the winds and the sea obey him" (Augustine, *Sermons*, 63.1-3).[1]

In his first inaugural address, Franklin D. Roosevelt uttered that famous line, "There is nothing to fear but fear itself." That isn't totally

| We should live fearlessly because we have the Lord of the storm within us. |

true. We fear God, and because we fear God, the fear of all but him fades away, and we live in boldness. We live in boldness knowing that the one we fear means us no harm. In fact, he went to the cross in perfect love to drive out fear.

Jesus is Lord of the storm. No blind fault, no hurricane, no parenting problem, feeling of loneliness, church problem, war, or sin is out of his control or out of his care. What storm is going on in your life? Let us awaken the Christ with the sound of our prayers, and ask for his healing. 3:16

---

[1]See Oden and Hall, *Mark*, 65.

Servants Like Jesus

1. What is your biggest fear?

2. What impact has fear had on your spiritual life over the years?

3. Why is it so hard to believe sometimes that "God is in control?"

4. Describe a time when you wondered whether God cared about what was going on in your life.

5. Tell the story of a time when God calmed a storm in your life.

Memory Verse
Philippians 4:6-7

Do not be anxious about anything, but in everything, by prayer and petition, with thanksgiving, present your requests to God. [7] And the peace of God, which transcends all understanding, will guard your hearts and your minds in Christ Jesus.

CHAPTER SIX

FAITH THAT RESCUES

MARK 5:21-43

Preston is a respectable man. He has a gorgeous wife, Linda, and daughter, Talitha—most people call her Tally. Preston drives a Mercedes and works as the chairman of his company. He has a membership at the most exclusive country club in town and is an elder at one of the city's most prominent congregations. Everyone loves Preston. He is a man of wisdom and is sought out for advice by many. He is humble, and though he has many diplomas and accomplishments to which he could point, he doesn't. He goes about his life with both excellence and humility.

Preston's life, to most, seems to be the stuff that dreams are made of. But Preston knows something that most people don't. His daughter, Tally, is getting sicker every day. Even the best doctors in the city can't figure out what the problem is. Tally has tried numerous medications. Preston and Linda have done as much personal research as they can. They stay up late every night surfing the net hoping they can find out what is causing little Tally to get sicker each day.

At church, they downplay what is wrong. "Oh, she's just a little sick," they say with a smile that satisfies both the nosy and genuinely concerned congregants. In their hearts, though, they know that Tally is more than a little sick. She is a lot sick.

One Sunday, when Preston and Linda get home from church, the paramedics are at the house. The babysitter says Tally just started convulsing. They take her to the hospital where she lays unconscious in bed. The sound of the heart monitor haunts the family as they gather and begin to pray.

The doctors still don't know what's wrong. They just know that if her fever gets much worse, she could be in real trouble. Preston and Linda ask the family for a moment alone. After they all depart, they stand there looking at their sweet little girl. Then, they go to their knees and pray like they never have before: "Father, we're afraid of what may happen. Tally is getting worse. Don't let her die. Please, God. Please do something."

> Then one of the synagogue rulers, named Jairus, came there. Seeing Jesus, he fell at his feet and pleaded earnestly with him, "My little daughter is dying. Please come and put your hands on her so that she will be healed and live." So Jesus went with him. A large crowd followed and pressed around him (Mark 5:22-24).

Worshiping in another church on the same day is Nadia. Nadia is a girl who had all of the fun she could while she was in college, which included binge drinking and promiscuity. Eventually she flunked out of SMU and went to work as a waitress at a dive bar on lower Greenville in Dallas. There, she continued to live the wildest of wild lives. Sometimes men would offer her drugs for sex, and she often accepted. Over time she developed a huge drug problem—heroin, LSD, acid, uppers, downers, the whole enchilada . . . she tried it all.

It seems like just yesterday she noticed these sores on her forearm. She went to the doctor to get them looked at. He broke the devastating news to her that she was HIV positive. She was absolutely, positively devastated. For a while, she thought that with all of the new advancement in HIV medication that she might be able to beat it. But over a three-year period her condition continued to decline. She realized that if she didn't do something soon, she was a goner.

So, in a final act of desperation, she decided to attend church. The greeters met her at the door and were cordial, but the sores on her face and arms drew their attention. When people at church asked, she said that she had been in a car accident. "Oh! Bless your heart," they said, and they looked relieved that it wasn't something worse.

Nadia still attends church today. She comes in 20 minutes late and makes sure that she leaves before church is out. She doesn't want to be seen. She covers herself in clothing from head to toe. She listens to the preaching and the praising, all the while praying the same prayer over and over: "God, if you are up there and can do it, please heal me." The healing she wants is healing from her disease, but more than that, she wants forgiveness for what she's done—the sex, the drugs, the partying, the harm to her parents and friends who tried to reach out to her to no avail. "I know you can do it . . . if you want to," she says to herself as the church stands to sing another song.

> And a woman was there who had been subject to bleeding for twelve years. She had suffered a great deal under the care of many doctors and had spent all she had, yet instead of getting better she grew worse. When she heard about Jesus, she came up behind him in the crowd and touched his cloak, because she thought, "If I just touch his clothes, I will be healed" (Mark 5:25-28).

People are people. Jairus and the woman subject to bleeding aren't ancient history. They are in our churches every week. In Mark 5 we read the stories of two *very* different people who come to Jesus looking for healing.

> **Jairus and the woman subject to bleeding aren't ancient history.**

Jesus' Healing Is Available to All

On this day, just like Preston and Nadia, Jairus and the woman with a hemorrhage are more alike than they know. Despite their many differences, both of them seek the same thing—the healing touch of Jesus. People are people to Jesus.

The two people who receive help from Jesus are at opposite ends of the socioeconomic and political spectrum. Jairus is a man of means (we can tell by the fact that he has a large household with messengers and the like). He is a synagogue ruler, a man of rank. In contrast to the woman with bleeding, he is given a name. The woman, on the other hand, is not given a name, and her complaint renders her ritually unclean. To put it in the words of one author, "She is walking pollution."[1] Mark adds that she comes to Jesus not rich like Jairus, but poor, having spent all she had seeking a cure for what ails her.

Mark dovetails the stories of these two dissimilar individuals to make the point that being male, ritually pure, holding a high religious office, or being a man of means provides no advantage in approaching Jesus. Likewise, being female, impure, dishonored, and destitute are no barrier to receiving help.[2]

If you saw the movie *Titanic*, you can't forget the last hour of the movie. Everyone on board knows the Titanic is going to sink. Accordingly, everyone scrambles to hop in a lifeboat so they can survive. There is only one problem: the Titanic was built with far fewer seats on lifeboats than there were passengers on board. That meant many would drown.

Can you remember how they decided who got on the lifeboats and who did not? The first people allowed a seat were the first-class passengers. Those who were not first-class were held back while the first-class passengers boarded the lifeboats. Women and children were next in line. In the end, if you were poor, older, and male, you were out of luck. It is a tough world where the difference between life and death is the price of a first-class ticket. To an extent, priority in antiquity was granted like it was on the Titanic. Praise be to God that the kingdom is not like that. Christ is the healer of all—rich and poor, male and female, old and young. Christ is the Great Healer because of his love and no other worldly standard. One of the implicit questions of the competing healings is: should Jesus bother stopping for a woman like this when he may endanger the life of one who is more worthy? The answer is, "Of course."

When it comes to dispensing grace, some today still make distinctions between clean and unclean, between worthiness and unworthiness. Take Preston and Nadia, for example. Who would you say deserves healing more? Preston has done nothing to get into the situation he is in. He seems to be the victim of simple bad luck. On the other hand, Nadia has done everything known to man to defile herself. She seems at least partially culpable in her malady. So if you were a friend of Preston's, and you, Preston, and Jesus were on your way to the hospital and Nadia came up and wanted to take up some of Jesus' time, how would you feel? Jesus knows the state of Jairus and the woman with bleeding. He heals them both because he loves them both. We don't earn God's love. God's love is freely given. Grace isn't given to the deserving. If it was, it wouldn't be grace, it would be payment.

Jesus doesn't set the lowly over against the lofty. Healing in the kingdom is not available only to the rich, nor is it only available to the poor. It is available not exclusively for the sinful, but also for the faithful. Mark is telling us through these stories that faith enables all: honored and dishonored, clean and unclean, rich and poor. *All are equal before Jesus.* The only thing that bonds Jairus and the bleeding woman together is that they have both heard about Jesus, are desperate for healing, and have run out of options. The need for Christ is more important than petty distinctions.

Interestingly, Jairus is a member of the Jewish establishment that seems on the whole to be hostile toward Jesus. Even Jairus' rank in a hostile institution does not disqualify him from Jesus' care because he is willing to lay aside whatever social status he has by humbling him-

> Grace isn't given to the deserving or it wouldn't be grace.

self before Jesus in a desperate plea for help. Jesus stands willing to answer the cries of both Jairus and the woman. In Jesus, healing is available to all.

> When she heard about Jesus, she came up behind him in the crowd and touched his cloak, because she thought, "If I just touch his clothes, I will be healed." Immediately her bleeding stopped and she felt in her body that she was freed from her suffering. At once Jesus realized that power had gone out from him. He turned around in the crowd and asked, "Who touched my clothes?" "You see the people crowding against you," his disciples answered, "and yet you can ask, 'Who touched me?'" But Jesus kept looking around to see who had done it. Then the woman, knowing what had happened to her, came and fell at his feet and, trembling with fear, told him the whole truth. He said to her, "Daughter, your faith has healed you. Go in peace and be freed from your suffering." While Jesus was still speaking, some men came from the house of Jairus, the synagogue ruler. "Your daughter is dead," they said. "Why bother the teacher any more?" Ignoring what they said, Jesus told the synagogue ruler, "Don't be afraid; just believe." He did not let anyone follow him except Peter, James and John the brother of James. When they came to the home of the synagogue ruler, Jesus saw a commotion, with people crying and wailing loudly. He went in and said to them, "Why all this commotion and wailing? The child is not dead but asleep." But they laughed at him. After he put them all out, he took the child's father and mother and the disciples who were with him, and went in where the child was. He took her by the hand and said to her, *"Talitha koum!"* (which means, "Little girl, I say to you, get up!"). Immediately the girl stood up and walked around (she was twelve years old) (Mark 5:27-42a).

Ministry in the Fast Lane

Perhaps this story speaks a word to us hurried people about how to deal with interruptions. One can only imagine how Jairus must have felt as Jesus stops to ask a question that even his disciples think is absurd as a little girl is in the process of dying. If you were Jairus, what might you be thinking? I might be thinking, "Hey, I was in line first!" And when I was told that my daughter was dead, I would have wondered how things might have been different if Jesus hadn't gotten tied up with that woman.

In the Gospel of Mark, Jesus is interrupted frequently. He is interrupted by Peter while he is praying (1:35-39), by a leper when he is preaching in the synagogue (1:40-45), by a paralytic when he is "speaking the word" (2:2), and by a sick woman while on his way to heal a dying girl in our text. The crowd rebukes an importunate blind beggar whose cry for help interrupts Jesus on his way up to Jerusalem on a mission that is, literally, crucial (10:48).

Jesus' power is put into the service of desperate and needy people. This doesn't mean that Jesus values them more than God or his mission. I simply mean that he understands that these "interruptions" have faces and names, and he loves them and cares for them. To Jesus, people aren't interruptions. They are those for whom he came to die.

> To Jesus, people aren't interruptions.

A teacher once remarked, "You know . . . my whole life I have been complaining that my work was constantly interrupted, until I discovered that my interruptions were my work."[3] I remember talking about how great college was except for the classes. And, I have heard many brethren speak as though church would be wonderful, if it weren't for the people. The church exists first for God, but then for his people.

Faith and Healing

Both Jairus and the bleeding woman are commended for their faith. In fact, in the case of the woman with bleeding, Jesus goes so far as to say, "Your faith has made you well." Neither Jairus nor the woman with bleeding come to faith *after* they are healed. They have faith in Jesus' ability to heal before he does it. Faith plays an important part in the healing process.

In Mark 5 we read how one appropriates the power of Jesus through faith. Faith can limp toward Jesus or run to Jesus. Faith comes in all shapes, sizes, and packages. Nevertheless, faith always summons the healing power of Jesus.

Having said that, we must acknowledge that evil, sickness, sin, and the death of little children continue to exist in our world. Not every touch heals, and those with faith still hear the dreaded word from the doctor, "Your little girl is dead." This story does not offer any explanation for why God allows evil to continue or exist or why the inexplicable still occurs. It does affirm that God is on the side of those who suffer and are stricken with grief. A miracle does not occur in every situation, but it does not lessen God's power to save. Rather, it beckons us to faith, just as it did when Jairus heard that his daughter had died. Jesus doesn't urge him not to be sad about it. He says, "Don't doubt, only believe."

> God is on the side of those who suffer.

Jairus' daughter, Little Tally, Talitha, was spared death for that day, but she was not given total reprieve. The woman with bleeding was healed that day, but she would face new ailments as she aged. Faith holds on in the face of death, knowing that God has conquered death in the resurrection of Christ. Jesus heals today and will raise the dead tomorrow. He is Lord of both the dead and the living. And, because he is, we live on in faith, awaiting the day when he will call our names and we will rise and join him in the place where is no bleeding or death— the place where all who have fallen on the mercy of Christ will gather—rich and poor, male and female, formerly sick and poor, now made whole and rich by the grace of God. [3:16]

---

[1]David Garland, *Mark*, The NIV Application Commentary (Grand Rapids: Zondervan, 1996) 224.

[2]See ibid., 225.

[3]See Lamar Williamson Jr., *Mark*, Interpretation Commentary (Atlanta: John Knox, 1983).

✞

C
H
A
P
T
E
R

6 *Faith That Rescues*

Servants Like Jesus

1. Who do you resemble more, Preston or Nadia? Jairus or the woman with bleeding?

2. What do we learn about Jesus' treatment of both people?

3. How can we do better at treating people equally?

4. Think of a time when hurriedness caused you to miss an opportunity for ministry. How does Jesus' treatment of the woman with bleeding provide insight for spiritual growth in this arena?

5. What advantage is there to acting righteously if grace is given to everyone according to their need?

6. Spend some time in prayer asking God for patience and mercy in dealing with those in need of healing.

> **Memory Verse**
> **Mark 5:35-36**
>
> *While Jesus was still speaking, some men came from the house of Jairus, the synagogue ruler. "Your daughter is dead," they said. "Why bother the teacher any more?" Ignoring what they said, Jesus told the synagogue ruler, "Don't be afraid; just believe."*

CHAPTER SEVEN

I'VE GOT SOME GOOD NEWS AND I'VE GOT SOME GOOD NEWS

MARK 8:27-38

The television ads for the 2004 presidential election got pretty ugly. Each commercial showed the scariest pictures of each candidate, with a creepy, Satan-like voiceover saying, "John Kerry did this; George Bush did this." All of it was an effort to discredit and shame the candidates.

Many years ago, the climate was similar. The word was out that there was a preacher who went around doing things that only prophets had done in the past. Lame people were walking again, the dead were even being raised, healings of all sorts were occurring. No one, not even his enemies, ever denied that Jesus' deeds occurred. They questioned *how* Jesus was capable of these things. Some said he was a prophet, some said he was doing it by the power of the devil. Others said that he was doing it because he was the Messiah.

Early in Mark chapter eight, Jesus provides food for 4,000 hungry people and restores sight to a blind man. Word continues to spread as Jesus and his disciples leave Galilee. We see a defining moment in the ministry of Jesus next as he clarifies in stark detail who he is.

> Jesus and his disciples went on to the villages around Caesarea Philippi. On the way he asked them, "Who do people say I am?" They replied, "Some say John the Baptist; others say Elijah; and still others, one of the prophets." "But what about you?" he asked. "Who do you say I am?" Peter answered, "You are the Christ"(Mark 8:27-29).

Who is Jesus? This question is one that society has relentlessly sought to answer. There are more entries in Encyclopedia Britannica that mention Jesus (over 20,000) than any other figure in history by far. Best-selling books like *The Da Vinci Code*, or *The God Gene: How Faith Is Hard-Wired into Our Genes*, try to answer the "Who is Jesus?" question, though they are misguided. Norman Mailer's book, *The Gospel according to the Son*, goes so far as to claim to be a fictitious personal memoir of Jesus. Charles Dickens, Leo Tolstoy, Nikos Kazantzakis, D.H. Lawrence, and countless others have tried to answer the Jesus question. None of these frequently accessed resources say what Scripture itself claims outright regarding his identity: he is the Christ.

Who is Jesus? He is the Christ.

Jesus never claims to be *a* way to God. He says that he is the *only* way to God. In John 14:6, he says, *"I am the way and the truth and the life. No one comes to the Father except through me."* The first step of faith is believing that statement—Jesus is the Messiah. He is the only way to God.

Some believe that all major religions basically say the same thing. The truth is they do ask similar questions: Who is God? Why is the world such a mess? How do we solve this problem? They do ask similar questions, but they come up with different answers. *Christianity is about God reaching out to humankind in Jesus Christ.* That is what Peter believed was true that day when he confessed that Jesus was more than a prophet. Jesus is *the Messiah*—the only one. This is gospel.

What "Messiah" Means

After Peter's remarkable confession, Jesus goes on to explain his destiny—crucifixion.

> He then began to teach them that the Son of Man must suffer many things and be rejected by the elders, chief priests and teachers of the law, and that he must be killed and after three days rise again. He spoke plainly about this, and Peter took him aside and began to rebuke him. But when Jesus turned and looked at his disciples, he rebuked Peter. "Get behind me, Satan!" he said. "You do not have in mind the things of God, but the things of men" (Mark 8:31-33).

Many Jews in Jesus' time believed that at some point in time God would intervene in human history through the Messiah. The Messiah would usher in the kingdom of God and its reign on this earth. Over time the Jews came to believe that the Messiah would lead their armies against the Romans, establishing a kingdom in Jerusalem of which God was king, and restoring the Temple to its proper place as the center of the world's religious life.

Jesus decisively rejected this. The role of Jesus as God's Anointed

‡

C
H
A
P
T
E
R

7

One meant that he would suffer, die, and rise. He wouldn't establish his glory and might through a dazzling military campaign against Rome. He would establish God's reign through humility, suffering, and death! It seldom occurs to us that greatness can come through servanthood rather than might. The teachers of Jesus' day had their vision of messiahship so firmly fixed in their heads that they would reject their Messiah before they would revise their expectations.

> It seldom occurs to us that greatness can come through servanthood rather than might.

Jesus was not put to death by the religious leaders of his day *in spite of* being the Messiah but *because* he was the Messiah! He was put to death because he was the anointed one of God, and that meant not earthly glory but self-sacrificial servanthood. Jesus lived to die for others! That's our Christ. That's our Messiah.

Messianic Living

Our belief that Jesus is the suffering servant Messiah shapes how we live as his followers.

> Then he called the crowd to him along with his disciples and said: "If anyone would come after me, he must deny himself and take up his cross and follow me. For whoever wants to save his life will lose it, but whoever loses his life for me and for the gospel will save it. What good is it for a man to gain the whole world, yet forfeit his soul? Or what can a man give in exchange for his soul?" (Mark 8:34-37).

Jesus says, "Lose your life and you will save it. If you try to save it, you will lose it." How does that work? That's so counterintuitive. Counterintuitive is an expression for something that is true even though it goes against our natural instincts. Our natural inclination is to believe the opposite of what Jesus says about self-denial holding the key to life. We like better the words of the well-known children's song about selfishness: finders keepers, losers weepers. That makes sense to us. Jesus turns it upside down and inside out: finders weepers, losers keepers!

We claim to be Christians, which means, "anointed ones." How should that impact how we live? As his anointed ones, we imitate he who came *"not to be served but to serve and to give his life as a ransom for many."* The purpose of our lives is to glorify God as a part of his family.

Jesus Christ gives us identity and becomes the lens through which we see the world. If you are a Christian, you are a Christian above all else. Before we are male or female, before we are black, white, or

Hispanic, we are Christians. We live for Jesus. That is what defines who we are.

> **If you are a Christian, you are a Christian above all else.**

A life lived for something as small as oneself is a miserable life. Jesus gives our lives meaning by calling us to something bigger than ourselves. Our greatest fear should not be failure but rather succeeding at something that doesn't really matter. Jesus calls us to something that matters. He calls us to imitate him.

When a family passes up the opportunity to buy a larger house to devote more of their financial blessings to God's work, this is "anointed" living. When a couple honors God in their physical relationship prior to marriage, this is anointed living. When the poor are cared for and the imprisoned are visited, this is anointed living. When churches are harangued for proclaiming God's standards in the world, this is anointed living. In reality, any time we give of ourselves for the sake of others, this is Messianic, or "anointed," living. This is the life Jesus lived.

We are Christians because we have fallen in love with Jesus. We have experienced God through him. Real Christians aren't Christians because they are afraid of the fires of hell. They aren't Christians because they need an emotional crutch or a hobby. Real Christians aren't Christians because of the fringe benefits of membership in the church. Christians are Christians because they believe in and have fallen in love with Jesus. 3:16

Servants Like Jesus

1. Why are you a Christian?

2. What is the biggest difference between Christianity and other religions?

3. In what ways have you suffered for Jesus?

4. What does Jesus mean when he says that those who lose their lives for his sake will find life, and those who seek to save their lives will lose their lives?

5. What do you love most about Jesus?

Then he called the crowd to him along with his disciples and said: "If anyone would come after me, he must deny himself and take up his cross and follow me. For whoever wants to save his life will lose it, but whoever loses his life for me and for the gospel will save it."

IT IS GOOD FOR US TO BE HERE

MARK 9:2-19

Aoccidrng to a rscreeah at Crmabdige Uinevtrisy, it denos't mtater in waht oredr the ltteers in a wrod are, the olny iprmonatt tinhg is taht the frsit and lsat lteter be at the rghit pacle. The rset can be a taotl mses and you can slitl raed it wotuhit porbelm. Tihs is bcuseae the huamn mnid deos not raed ervey lteter by istlef, but the wrod as a wlohe.

The human mind is an amazing thing. It has the capacity to mathematically organize things, recognize objects, and sort out letters, numbers, and even sounds. However, the mind's wonderful capacity to recognize and sort sound leads to a phenomenon that we in America affectionately refer to as *selective hearing*.

Dale Carnegie said that hearing one's name is the most beautiful sound to the human ear. There are other sounds, voices and instructions that we simply would rather not hear, and therefore choose not to.

No matter at what decibel level a request is given, kids can always fail to hear Mom calling them away from the basketball game for dinner. Husbands miraculously fail to hear instructions to pick up socks and towels. This is selective hearing.

Throughout the course of our lives we all develop this remarkable talent. More often than not, this talent carries over into the spiritual realm. We listen to God on some occasions, particularly when his words are easy listening. This isn't usually premeditated or malicious. Some parts of God's Word are simply easier to hear than others.

Selective spirituality often creeps in without our noticing. It even happened to Peter.

You will remember that just after Peter confessed his faith in Jesus that Jesus told him that he must suffer and die. Peter refused to accept the news. He would hear none of it.

On this particular day, Peter is taken, with James and John, and given a special glimpse into God. Peter would need his ears. He would need his eyes. He would need his imagination. He could have done without his mouth. But, then again, it is always easier to listen selectively than it is to speak selectively.

> After six days Jesus took Peter, James and John with him and led them up a high mountain, where they were all alone. There he was transfigured before them. His clothes became dazzling white, whiter than anyone in the world could bleach them. And there appeared before them Elijah and Moses, who were talking with Jesus. Peter said to Jesus, "Rabbi, it is good for us to be here. Let us put up three shelters—one for you, one for Moses and one for Elijah." (He did not know what to say, they were so frightened.) Then a cloud appeared and enveloped them, and a voice came from the cloud: "This is my Son, whom I love. Listen to him!" Suddenly, when they looked around, they no longer saw anyone with them except Jesus. As they were coming down the mountain, Jesus gave them orders not to tell anyone what they had seen until the Son of Man had risen from the dead. They kept the matter to themselves, discussing what "rising from the dead" meant (Mark 9:2-10).

Who can really blame Peter? To see Moses, Elijah, and Jesus together in their glory must have been completely overwhelming. As his jaw hangs open in utter amazement, Peter is speechless. Unfortunately he doesn't stay speechless.

> Peter is speechless. Unfortunately he doesn't stay that way.

In his excitement (literally, "terror") Peter suggests that three tents be built—one for Moses, one for Elijah, and one for Jesus. His idea brings a voice from heaven that thunders, "This is my beloved Son, whom I love. Listen to him!"

Listen to Jesus!

I don't know that I would have done any better on that occasion. The text says that Peter didn't know what to say, and I'm not sure I would have either. It's easy for me to look back and say, "Well, I would have known exactly what to say," but when in the presence of something that awesome, we would all have been speechless.

Moses and Elijah testified to the coming of the Christ, but they themselves were not the Christ. Jesus is Lord of all. Jesus is Lord over Moses *and* Elijah. He doesn't share worship with others. It is inappropriate to honor them equally.

It is easy for us to acquit ourselves of the sin of idolatry because we believe that idolatry is a sin people in antiquity committed, or that one must renounce one's faith in God to engage in idolatry. In Scripture, idolatry is identified as such when Israel worships Yahweh *and* Baal, or Yahweh *and* other gods.

Idolatry not only happens today but it happens every day. Just as Peter, we too often build more tents than there should be. We don't turn our back on God altogether. Nor, are we even conscious that we are worshiping anything other than God. *Here's a question: If Moses and Elijah pale in comparison to Jesus, how badly do our idols pale in comparison to Jesus?*

Peter meant well. Awestruck by the grandeur of Jesus alongside the representatives of the law and its preaching, it seemed totally appropriate to build three tents. Perhaps Peter even planned to reserve the best tent for Jesus. It would have the best carpet, granite countertops, crown molding, a four-car garage, and a hot tub.

> Jesus doesn't want the best tent. He wants the only tent.

Here's the thing, though: Jesus doesn't want the best tent. **He wants the only tent.** He doesn't want us to build a tent for Jesus and tents for Moses and Elijah. He doesn't want us to build a tent for Jesus and a tent for status or America or even to our children. Anything that competes with Jesus for supremacy in our lives is an idol. They beckon a voice from heaven saying, "This is my Son, whom I love. Listen to him!"

Jesus is not one among other people or things that are worthy of worship. He alone is worthy of worship, and he alone is the source of our doctrine and practice. He alone is to be our heart's desire.

A Call to Worship

The story of the transfiguration has something to say to us about how awesome and crucial the presence of God is for disciples. God's presence exposes our idolatry and reminds us who we serve. When confronted with the glorious vision of Christ, the Bible says that, "Peter didn't know what to say."

When was the last time the presence of God left you speechless? If it has been a while, let me offer you a few reasons why that may be the case.

> When was the last time the presence of God left you speechless?

Sometimes we are just too busy for God. Imagine if Peter declined to go to the mountaintop with Christ because of his busy schedule. How ridiculous does that sound? Yet, there are places that God wants to take us, places he wants to show us, words he wants to say to us, if we will make ourselves available for it. Macrina Wiederkehr makes the point:

> Spending your days in the fast lane of life impairs the quality of your seeing. If you want to see to the depths, you will need to slow down. You live in a world of theophanies. Holiness comes wrapped in the ordinary. There are burning bushes all around you. Every tree is full of angels. Hidden beauty is waiting in every crumb. Life wants to lead you from crumbs to angels, but this can happen only if you are willing to unwrap the ordinary by staying with it long enough to harvest its treasure."[1]

God wants to know us and to be known by us. What a blessing!

First Thessalonians 5:19 urges us, "Do not put out the Spirit's fire." The Spirit's fire is what fuels the Christian life and provides a sense of God's presence. Many things can pour water on the Spirit's fire. Sin in our lives can do it. In other cases, people never experience the true power of God's presence because they don't believe in his power. Everyone who has ever found themselves in God's presence has been absolutely amazed. They might be left speechless or fall on their faces, but no one ever leaves God's presence unchanged or bored. Those who have spent years walking with God can tell you that life with God isn't one big mountaintop. There are peaks, valleys, and flatlands. Some parts of the journey are more interesting or beautiful than others. However, this we can be sure of: the presence of God transforms the human life.

A Call to Mission

Genuine faith immersed daily in the presence of God will inevitably lead us toward sharing Jesus with others. Notice that in verse 9, Jesus tells the disciples: "Don't tell anyone until I have risen." Why would he say that? Because he knew that the vision of his radiance and glory was so amazing that they would be dying to tell others.

A lack of evangelistic fervor in a life or in a church often has less to do with an intentional neglect of the great commission than it does a lack of the power and presence of God. The transformation that we experience as we live with God fills us with boldness to share our faith and compassion for those who don't know Christ. If the power and presence of God isn't real in our lives and churches, evangelism will be an afterthought at best, and a distant memory at worst.

In Scripture, evangelism is done, without exception, by two types of people: new converts and mature disciples. Conspicuously absent from the Bible are stories of conversion by the lukewarm. As John, who was there on the mountaintop that day would say later, "That which was from the beginning, which we have heard, which we have seen with our eyes, which we have looked at and our hands have touched—this we proclaim concerning the Word of life" (1 John 1:1). Jesus took his disciples to the mountain that day so that they could experience his presence in a new way. God wants every person to experience his presence.

When the vision dissipated, the text says that "They saw no one but Jesus." May we see no one but Jesus. And, may we be left speechless by God so that we may speak about him to those whom God also wants to lead up his holy mountain. 3:16

---

[1]Macrina Wiederkehr, *A Tree Full of Angels* (New York: HarperCollins, 1990) xii-xiii.

It Is Good for Us to Be Here 8

Servants Like Jesus

1. What do you think you would have said if you saw what Peter did on the mountaintop?

2. What is idolatry? Name some contemporary idols.

3. What besides Jesus do you attempt to build a tent for in your life?

4. Describe a "mountaintop" experience you have had with God.

5. Pray that God will grant you "a constant sense of his abiding presence."

Memory Verse Mark 9:7-8 | *Then a cloud appeared and enveloped them, and a voice came from the cloud: "This is my Son, whom I love. Listen to him!" Suddenly, when they looked around, they no longer saw anyone with them except Jesus.*

Chapter Nine

Help My Unbelief

MARK 9:14-29

When they came to the other disciples, they saw a large crowd around them and the teachers of the law arguing with them. As soon as all the people saw Jesus, they were overwhelmed with wonder and ran to greet him. "What are you arguing with them about?" he asked. A man in the crowd answered, "Teacher, I brought you my son, who is possessed by a spirit that has robbed him of speech. Whenever it seizes him, it throws him to the ground. He foams at the mouth, gnashes his teeth and becomes rigid. I asked your disciples to drive out the spirit, but they could not." "O unbelieving generation," Jesus replied, "how long shall I stay with you? How long shall I put up with you? Bring the boy to me." So they brought him. When the spirit saw Jesus, it immediately threw the boy into a convulsion. He fell to the ground and rolled around, foaming at the mouth. Jesus asked the boy's father, "How long has he been like this?" "From childhood," he answered. "It has often thrown him into fire or water to kill him. But if you can do anything, take pity on us and help us." "'If you can'?" said Jesus. "Everything is possible for him who believes." Immediately the boy's father exclaimed, "I do believe; help me overcome my unbelief!" When Jesus saw that a crowd was running to the scene, he rebuked the evil spirit. "You deaf and mute spirit," he said, "I command you, come out of him and never enter him again." The spirit shrieked, convulsed him violently and came out. The boy looked so much like a corpse that many said, "He's dead." But Jesus took him by the hand and lifted him to his feet, and he stood up. After Jesus had gone indoors, his disciples asked him privately, "Why couldn't we drive it out?" He replied, "This kind can come out only by prayer" (Mark 9:14-29).

t is one thing to endure suffering; it is quite another to watch someone you love suffer. It is even more severe to watch your children suffer. To watch a child suffer may be the most excruciating form of suffering there is. We cannot help but feel this father's pain. His son has a demon, which paralyzes him, causes him to foam at the mouth, grind his teeth, and throw himself into the fire or into the water in an effort to kill himself. Worst of all, he has lost his ability to speak.

As a father it must have been so hard. His son, perhaps once happy and active is now the one people talk about under their breath when they see him. His son is one the other parents don't want their kids going near.

This father has come to the apostles in hopes that they can heal his son. Try as they might, they cannot. The teachers of the law in a typical display of pastoral sensitivity and timing, begin to ridicule the apostles as false prophets and bunk witchdoctors. Just then, Peter, James, John, and Jesus arrive—fresh from the mount of Transfiguration. Suddenly the bickering stops and a grieving father makes one last attempt to see his son healed.

Jesus asks what the fight is about. He is told about his disciples' inabilities. The boy's father jumps in, "If you can, Lord, heal him." Jesus is underwhelmed by the father's faith and thus reminds him that everything is possible for those who believe. The father cries out in desperation, "I believe—help my unbelief." Jesus honors his prayer.

The evil spirit shrieks as the boy convulses and falls as though dead. But Jesus heals him completely of his infirmity. What a moment it must have been when after those years of separation, the boy who had been separated from the Lord was grasped by the hand and raised from his spiritual death. What a moment that would have been to see the father embrace his son, now in his right mind, and say, "I love you, Son."

Real Faith

The boy's father is a role model for us. Obviously, his faith isn't limitless. Yet he prayed with whatever faith he had, and asked God to provide the faith he didn't have. Such is the essence of real faith. Real faith is humble enough to admit when it is wanting, and hopeful enough to trust that God can provide the faith that is needed.

> The boy's father is a role model for us.

This is a story about faith, and particularly how faith works when the rubber meets the road—both when we ourselves are seeking healing, and when we are in the fields of ministry as disciples. Faith is not a theory. Faith is not logic. Faith is not optimism. Faith is a journey in which we believe the power of God and demonstrate its power by how we live. The Canadian literary critic Northrop Frye once said correctly that ". . . faith is not anything we say or believe, or that we think we believe, or that we believe we believe. What we really believe is what our actions show that we believe."[1]

This father demonstrates his faith in both the bringing of his son to Jesus and the beauty of his prayer, which despite what appears to be a lack of faith on the surface, displays a humility of spirit that the disciples and religious leaders appear to lack.

The word of gospel in this story is not that Jesus demands faith from his disciples, though he does. It is that he supplies faith where our faith runs out. This is a good thing, for there are times in life when we are confronted with spiritual questions that feel too big for us to overcome. There are loved ones that we feel powerless to help. In those times, we can turn to Jesus in our need of faith, and he will supply it.

The Great Faithkiller

Initially the boy's father tries to bring his son to Jesus. Jesus isn't available, so he is forced to settle for the apostles. This normally would not be a problem. Jesus had empowered the apostles to cast out demons (Mark 3:15; 6:7). They even had some experience with success (6:13-14). However, in this case, they look like amateur magicians unable to make the rabbit come out of the hat. This brings the criticism of the teachers of the law who are dying to point out that, if they were disciples of the true Messiah, they would be able to accomplish this healing. This causes an argument, and togas are in a twist.

Despite the wonder of the miracle that Jesus performs and the beauty of the father's prayer, *the focal point of this story as it is told in Mark is the shortcomings of the disciples.* This story is recorded in Matthew, Mark, and Luke. Yet, only Mark records the fight between the disciples and the religious leaders. Why does he tell us about this? Could it be that Mark wants us to be aware of the frivolity of pettiness?

Imagine what the father of the sick boy was thinking as he stood there watching the spat between the apostles and religious leaders. He has a son whom he can't speak to who is trying to kill himself. He convulses, foams at the mouth, and throws himself into both fire and water. If I were that father, I might be thinking, "Is this all you can do? Fight? What about my son?"

Too often the church misses great opportunities for witness and ministry because of petty fighting. The disciples and religious leaders wrangle with their opponents while a father stands by agonizing over his suffering son. Sometimes people come to Christ's followers for help and they get trivial arguments instead. Some churches spend more time arguing than helping anybody or praying. This doesn't honor Christ.

> Some churches spend more time arguing than helping or praying.

Jesus' first question upon arriving, "What are you arguing with them about?" should be called to mind every time we are tempted to divert attention from the mission of God to argue about matters of lesser importance.

Ministry in the Middle Miles

Any person or church taking mountains for God should prepare for attacks from all sides. Jesus' disciples experience a great truth on this day: maturity in Christ does not make the journey easier—and we do not become more self-sufficient. True disciples are always dependent on the power of God for ministry. These truths become especially important as we enter the "middle miles" of our Christian journey.

Like a marathon, the Christian race is most difficult to run in the middle miles. At the beginning, we have the cheering of loved ones and friends to inspire us—as well as a fresh set of spiritual lungs. Toward the end of our lives we can see the finish line, and are inspired by the vision of crossing the finish line and the heavenly banquet that awaits us. However, those middle miles can be hard. The middle miles are when cheers are drowned out by the sound of our panting. Our lungs burn, our legs grow weak, and the end is nowhere in sight.

This is where the disciples are. They have been empowered by Jesus and have spent a while healing and doing his work. They have turned a corner in their pilgrimage and now it's getting harder. So their faith is getting tested in the crucible of real ministry, not in the comfort of a campfire discussion about faith. They are in the middle miles now.

> Those middle miles can be hard.

Such is life as a disciple. As we learn to walk with Jesus, we are given harder and more meaningful tasks which will demand more courage, more energy, and as we learn today . . . more faith. At some point, we will fall short of what we hope to accomplish. God uses these times to welcome us back to reliance on his power to do more than we ever can without it.

Only through Prayer

The disciples fail on this occasion, apparently for lack of faith and prayer. Mark tells us: *"After Jesus had gone indoors, his disciples asked him privately, 'Why couldn't we drive it out?' He replied, 'This kind can come out only by prayer'"* (Mark 9:28-29). It could be that the disciples had become like the other exorcists of their time. No devotion to the deity was required—just as the one who possessed Aladdin's lamp needed only rub it to get the three wishes.

Middle-mile ministry can easily become mechanical. When preachers preach without prayer or time spent with the Bible, people suffer. When elders become mere managers without cultivating a Christlike love for the church and people, in prayer, people suffer. When Christians choose consumerism over discipleship, people suffer.

In the middle miles, let us not drift from dependence on God to self-reliance or confidence. Mark is suggesting that self-confidence and optimism may feel like faith, but they aren't. The attitude of "I believe—help my unbelief" is necessary for the healer as well as the sufferer. Really high-impact ministry can only be done through prayer. This is because, as Henri Nouwen has asserted, prayer, *"is a way of being empty and useless in the presence of God and so of proclaiming our basic belief that all is grace and nothing is simply the result of hard work."*[2]

Whatever talents or gifts we may possess, God is the source of whatever power goes forth from our ministry. The disciples were reminded of this when they lost their influence that day. I hope that we don't have to learn *that* lesson *that* way. God wants to increase our spiritual influence. As long as we stay on our knees, relying on God to do ministry through us, "all things are possible for those who believe" (9:23).

> God is the source of whatever power goes forth from our ministry.

---

[1] Northrop Frye, cited in Peter Gomes, *The Good Life: Truths That Last in Times of Need* (San Francisco: HarperSanFrancisco, 2002) 265.

[2] Henri Nouwen, quoted in Garland, *Mark*, 362.

Servants Like Jesus

1. Describe a time when petty fights hindered ministry.

2. If God were not a part of your life, how would it be different?

3. Think of a time when your faith felt insufficient. How did you respond?

4. Northrop Frye said, "We believe what our actions say that we believe." Do you agree or disagree?

5. What do your actions say that you believe?

Memory Verse Mark 9:28-29	*After Jesus had gone indoors, his disciples asked him privately, "Why couldn't we drive it out?" He replied, "This kind can come out only by prayer."*

CHAPTER TEN

THOSE WHO ARE NOT AGAINST US ARE FOR US

MARK 9:38-50

"Teacher," said John, "we saw a man driving out demons in your name and we told him to stop, because he was not one of us."

"Do not stop him," Jesus said. "No one who does a miracle in my name can in the next moment say anything bad about me, for whoever is not against us is for us. I tell you the truth, anyone who gives you a cup of water in my name because you belong to Christ will certainly not lose his reward.

"And if anyone causes one of these little ones who believe in me to sin, it would be better for him to be thrown into the sea with a large millstone tied around his neck. If your hand causes you to sin, cut it off. It is better for you to enter life maimed than with two hands to go into hell, where the fire never goes out. And if your foot causes you to sin, cut it off. It is better for you to enter life crippled than to have two feet and be thrown into hell. And if your eye causes you to sin, pluck it out. It is better for you to enter the kingdom of God with one eye than to have two eyes and be thrown into hell, where

"'their worm does not die,
and the fire is not quenched.'
Everyone will be salted with fire.

"Salt is good, but if it loses its saltiness, how can you make it salty again? Have salt in yourselves, and be at peace with each other" (Mark 9:38-50).

Most disciples are confronted at one point or another of their spiritual journey with the issue of where to draw the lines. Most of us will wonder at some point, "Who's in? Who's out?" This was John's day to deal with this tough question. It seems like just moments ago that John was standing on the mountaintop with Jesus blazing in glory alongside Moses and Elijah. To a reader of Mark, the words of God's voice from heaven at the Transfiguration are fresh: "This is my son whom I love, listen to him."

John is not a Johnny-come-lately. He is often referred to as the apostle whom Jesus loved. Thus we can't just easily dismiss him as one on the far right wing of the movement. John is at the core of what Jesus is trying to do on earth. John loves Jesus and wants to do right by Jesus.

Such is the case with most sectarians. Most of the sectarians I know are devoted followers. They don't want to damage anyone (usually) or bring shame to Christ's name. They don't intend to damage the church's witness. These are not John's intentions either. So John tells an exorcist who is carrying out his ministry in Jesus' name to stop. Why? "Because he wasn't one of us" (9:38). Jesus rebukes John. For Jesus, intentions aren't everything. What matters most to Jesus are his mission and the unity of believers.

Roots of Sectarianism

Pride

At its root, sectarianism is often a sin of pride. It might be a simple pride that enjoys being a part of a group one thinks is more special, or has cornered the market on truth. It simply feels good to belong to the most exclusive country club in town, graduate from an ivy league university, or belong to the right fraternity. The sense of gratification that these things bring is insignificant when compared with the sense of pride we can enjoy when we believe we are the only right ones with regard to doctrine and faith.

Throughout Mark 9, Mark goes out of his way to point out the pride of the disciples. Earlier in the chapter the apostles are arguing about who is the greatest among them. Now they are excluding others from ministry because they are not part of their group. Perhaps they felt as though they were the only one's capable of healing, so others could be phonies. Most Christian sectarians also believe that those who practice differently or think differently do so out of either ignorance or dishonesty.

Jealousy

There is more to the disciples' sectarianism than meets the eye. When we read all of Mark 9, we remember that the disciples had earlier tried to exorcise a demon and couldn't do it. Get this: now the disciples tell this person to stop doing something that they themselves weren't able to do. The apostles tried to the best of their ability to exorcise the demon, but they couldn't do it. Now, they stop one who is able to exorcise demons because he is not one of them. What irony. What pride. What jealousy. And so Jesus looks at John, the one whom he loves, and he says, "Don't tell him to stop."

When I was twelve, I competed in a junior golf tournament against Tiger Woods. Yes, *the* Tiger Woods. My two friends and I had heard about this kid from Cypress who called himself "Tiger." We had played pretty well over the course of the tournament and thus had been paired with him in the final foursome on the final day. I'm sure he was terrified! We heckled him on the driving range and pulled against him on every shot. When he shot about twelve strokes lower than we did on the day, I can remember us sitting around bellyaching about how the course favored his style of game. We simply couldn't cheer for someone other than ourselves. We couldn't be happy for him or admit that he played well. One of my buddies who played in the foursome that day still believes that he would be as good a golfer as Tiger if he had kept practicing. He still believes that Tiger isn't *that* good! He is guilty of more than delusion. He remains jealous.

Christians sometimes exclude one another or refuse to work together when the basis for sectarianism comes only from the simple but pungent vice of jealousy. We must always make sure that we do not separate from other Christians out of jealousy. In times like these, Christians need to celebrate one another's victories. We need to rejoice that there are others who are accomplishing things for Jesus that we might not be able to. We should never pull against them or tell them to stop because they aren't part of us.

In Dallas where I'm blessed to live and preach, there are so many Christian churches that it is quite common for churches to speak poorly of one another and secretly pull against

> Christians need to celebrate one another's victories.

one another in hopes of attracting one another's members. This surely sickens Christ and taints our effectiveness as his followers.

It was a great day for me when I realized my "tribe" was not the only one who believed in the sanctity of God's Word and who was sold out for the cause of Christ. I realized that some of the best preaching, writing, church planting, teaching, scholarship, etc., was being done by others who were not part of my group. I came to the conclusion that if someone was doing Jesus' ministry in Jesus' name I would not tell them to stop. As Jesus says in Mark 9:40, "those who are not against us are for us." This is nothing to be afraid of. This is gospel.

A Plea for Unity

We all understand that we can't throw truth out for the sake of unity, but we should acknowledge that unity is a core doctrine of the Bible. As Paul says in Ephesians 4:3, "Make every effort to keep the **unity** of the Spirit through the bond of peace."

There is a spiritual war taking place in the world right now. In wartime we don't have the luxury of picking our battle buddies. We should just be glad that they are not shooting at us. This is Jesus' point to John in Mark 9:39. Jesus says, "No one who does a miracle in my name can in the next moment say anything bad about me." I don't know about you, but I am glad that there are those outside my tribe who won't turn against Jesus quickly. What a blessing! It is indeed wonderful to know that God's kingdom doesn't rise and fall on the back of my congregation or my fellowship. There are others out there who are not going to deny Christ quickly. This is something to be thankful for.

> The church has a peacetime mentality.

Spiritually speaking, this is wartime. But here's the truth: *the church has a peacetime mentality*. Division is a luxury of the majority in peacetime. Many Christians do not *really* believe that there is an evil presence in this world that is trying to destroy Christ's body. Jesus knows better. So should we. These are times that call for unity. As a friend of mine once pointed out to me, "It's one thing for soldiers to fight in the barracks over a card game in peacetime, it's another for them to fight with one another in the trenches when there is a battle on."

We are in a spiritual war. It is dangerous for us not to sense this. On that terrible day of September 11, 2001, we learned that it is possible to be at war and not know it. Satan means business, and that is why Paul urges us to take every piece of armor we can get our hands on: helmets, shields, belts, and everything else God has graciously provided us—including the fellowship of millions of Christ-followers all over the globe.

Concerns about doctrine are valid and crucial to the purity of the church. Nevertheless, we must also understand that unity is sound doc-

> Unity is sound doctrine.

trine, and that we are to leave be those who are doing Jesus' ministry in his name. He doesn't say we have to look exactly alike, he just says don't stop them, leave them alone.

The Lord blessed me with the opportunity to spend a summer on a short-term mission project to Bangkok, Thailand. Thailand is more than 90% Buddhist. If you walk into any convenience store, you will see a Buddha behind the counter with incense burning next to it. Buddha is everywhere.

Throughout the summer, I slept in the same room with nine other guys. Two slept on the floor, while the rest of us slept in beds. There was no air conditioning even though the temperature never dropped below 90 degrees the whole time we were there. And let me say it was not a dry heat.

Next to us was a room full of girls who were equally crowded. The young men and women were all there for the same reason. Their families had thrown them out of their homes and disowned them for becoming Christians. There at the edge of Bangkok's largest university, which has approximately 300,000 Buddhist students, is the little student center where about twenty Christians live.

Sunday morning worship is different there. You get up in the morning, have Bible class, and then worship time. Afterwards everybody goes out to the courtyard and makes food for one another. They eat lunch together, and then they play games until about 4:00 p.m. when they have another Bible hour. The Thai Christians study Scripture together and then they make and eat food together again.

When I saw this way of doing Sundays, I will confess that I thought to myself, "My goodness, folks, don't you have a life?" The answer is, "yes." They have *real* life. Christianity *is* their life. The Thai form of Christianity is puzzling to those of us used to looking at our watches after an hour of being together on Sundays. This is because the passion of their community has been forged by persecution and life as aliens and strangers in a country. Ours generally has not. Over the next several weeks I was blessed to experience the richness of Christian community lived in lonelier circumstances than those I live through in Dallas, Texas. Sectarianism is a luxury of those of us who live in a country in which Christians are the majority and few, if any, genuine persecutions exist. Everyone ought to see first hand what God is doing overseas because it reminds us how awesome he is and how vast his work in the world is.

My view of other Christian groups evolved further when our mission team went to see the largest golden Buddha in the world at Wat Traimit. The statue is over 15 feet tall, over 13 feet wide, and weighs over 5 tons. We stared in amazement at the extravagance of the statue while hundreds of people worshiped it. In six weeks I hadn't seen another Christian other than those at the local Thai church. I got a sinking feeling inside that I can only describe as "spiritual loneliness."

I was overwhelmed with sorrow as I watched these hundreds worshiping Buddha. Just then a group of American students walked in. One

Those Who Are Not against Us Are for Us 10

of the girls was wearing a T-shirt that said, "Baptist Student Union." I had never been so glad to see a Baptist in all my life! I said a quick prayer, "Thank you, Lord." In a place like Bangkok, it is amazing how clear it is who the enemy is not.

I wonder why it takes persecution for us to embrace this truth? We must embrace the values that Jesus laid out for John that day: those

> **Why does it take persecution for us to embrace this truth?**

who are not against us are for us. Don't tell them to stop; don't compete with them. Instead, those who are doing Jesus' ministry in the name of Jesus are to be viewed as friends, not enemies.

Unity Brings Hope and Victory

The stirring of unity in the church is something that makes Satan tremble with fear because a united church is something against which his gates cannot prevail. For too long, Satan's gates have stood strong, as an anemic and underweight church knocked politely on its doors. But the time has come for the church to storm Hell's gates together. If we do, his gates don't have a chance.

There was a time when Christians gave heart and soul to keep the unity of the spirit through the bond of peace. Are those days gone? I am thankful that by God's grace, the answer to that is "no." In unprecedented ways, Christians are working together to keep the unity of the spirit by rebuilding burned bridges. As we do, Satan's knees knock, and God's power readies.

Jesus says that we will be recognized as his if we love one another. John got it that day. When he penned his retelling of the life of Jesus, he recalled and recorded this beautiful prayer of Jesus:

> My prayer is not for them alone. I pray also for those who will believe in me through their message, that all of them may be one, Father, just as you are in me and I am in you. May they also be in us so that the world may believe that you have sent me. I have given them the glory that you gave me, that they may be one as we are one: I in them and you in me. May they be brought to complete unity to let the world know that you sent me and have loved them even as you have loved me (John 17:20-23).

Later, John would help us understand that loving one another is essential to right relationship with God.

> Dear friends, let us love one another, for love comes from God. Everyone who loves has been born of God and knows God. Whoever does not love does not know God, because God is love (1 John 4:7-8).

Sectarianism is a spiritual disease that infects virtually every branch of the Christian faith. Truth is the pillar of all right doctrine. It is the pillar of the Christian faith. Jesus isn't calling us to jettison the truth for the sake of unity. However, he defines truth differently than I think some have in the past. He says, "I am the truth. Stand for that. I am the truth. And so plant your feet there." We must make that the place where you break your fellowship. You do it based on the truth. The truth who is Jesus Christ.

If the divinity of Christ, the power of the Spirit, the existence of God is at issue, the situation becomes different because unity must abide in truth. However, Jesus would have us know that unity is at the very heart of right doctrine. Unity and discipleship are married. They cannot be divorced.

So where do we begin? We begin by committing to unity with one another and to glorifying Christ in ministry together. We allow God to drive out fear of those who are not of our group and ask him to replace it with respect and joy that there are others who are on our side in this work against the principalities of the evil one. Then, we together storm the gates of Hell which simply cannot prevail against the united people of God. What a vision! What a Savior!

Those Who Are Not against Us Are for Us 10

Servants Like Jesus

1. Define sectarianism.

2. The author lists pride and jealousy as two roots of sectarianism. Can you name some others?

3. What have you done to further unity among believers? What more can you do?

4. What signs do you see that there is a spiritual war on?

5. Describe a time when you felt "spiritually lonely."

6. Pray the prayer of Jesus from John 17. What verse from that prayer inspires you most?

Memory Verse
Mark 9:38-40

"Teacher," said John, "we saw a man driving out demons in your name and we told him to stop, because he was not one of us." "Do not stop him," Jesus said. "No one who does a miracle in my name can in the next moment say anything bad about me, for whoever is not against us is for us."

CHAPTER ELEVEN

CLEANSING THE TEMPLE

MARK 11:12-25

The next day as they were leaving Bethany, Jesus was hungry. Seeing in the distance a fig tree in leaf, he went to find out if it had any fruit. When he reached it, he found nothing but leaves, because it was not the season for figs. Then he said to the tree, "May no one ever eat fruit from you again." And his disciples heard him say it. On reaching Jerusalem, Jesus entered the temple area and began driving out those who were buying and selling there. He overturned the tables of the money changers and the benches of those selling doves, and would not allow anyone to carry merchandise through the temple courts. And as he taught them, he said, "Is it not written: 'My house will be called a house of prayer for all nations'? But you have made it 'a den of robbers.'" The chief priests and the teachers of the law heard this and began looking for a way to kill him, for they feared him, because the whole crowd was amazed at his teaching. When evening came, they went out of the city. In the morning, as they went along, they saw the fig tree withered from the roots. Peter remembered and said to Jesus, "Rabbi, look! The fig tree you cursed has withered!" "Have faith in God," Jesus answered. "I tell you the truth, if anyone says to this mountain, 'Go, throw yourself into the sea,' and does not doubt in his heart but believes that what he says will happen, it will be done for him. Therefore I tell you, whatever you ask for in prayer, believe that you have received it, and it will be yours. And when you stand praying, if you hold anything against anyone, forgive him, so that your Father in heaven may forgive you your sins" (Mark 11:12-25).

The cursing of the fig tree and the cleansing of the Temple are two of Jesus' most frequently misunderstood actions. This is no surprise, for on their own, these two events are very difficult to understand. When read together, however, these two events explain each other.

Mark wants us to know as much. You see, throughout his biography of Jesus, Mark uses a "sandwich technique," where he begins telling a story, begins a different story, and then comes back and finishes the first story. In chapter eleven, Mark begins telling the story of Jesus cursing the fig tree. He then interrupts that story to describe Jesus driving out the money changers from the Temple. Only then does he return to the story of the fig tree. This is Mark's way of telling us that these two events are related to each other. Mark is telling us that if we miss the meaning of the fig tree, we may miss the meaning of the clearing out of the Temple as well.

> Mark is telling us that these two events are related to each other.

In Season and Out of Season

If you went to a major league baseball park in December looking for a game, you wouldn't find one. December isn't baseball season. People don't go skiing in August. August isn't ski season. Mark tells us at the beginning of the narrative that it isn't fig season. The fig tree is doing nothing wrong. It is doing exactly what most would say it should be doing. So why does Jesus curse the tree?

Commenting on this text, a scholar by the name of Klausner calls the cursing of the fig tree, "a gross injustice on a tree which was guilty of no wrong and had but performed its natural function."[1] Another scholar by the name of Manson (no relation to Marilyn or Charles), comments: "It is a tale of miraculous power wasted in the service of ill-temper (for the supernatural energy employed to blast the unfortunate tree might have been more usefully expended in forcing a crop of figs out of season); and as it stands is simply incredible."[2]

On the surface it may seem as though they have a point. Does Jesus have anything to teach us here other than how to lose our tempers? The answer is, "absolutely," but the life-changing lesson lies amidst the overturned tables of the Temple. The story of the cursing of the fig tree doesn't end there; Mark will pick it up again after he tells us about the Temple cleansing. Remember that these stories (the cursing of the fig tree and the Temple cleansing) are meant to interpret one another.

Cleansing the Temple

We get a picture of what is irking Jesus from the two passages of Scriptures he quotes. The first one is Isaiah 56:7, "My house shall be a house of prayer for all nations." The next passage Jesus quotes is Jeremiah 7:9-11, "Will you steal and murder, commit adultery and perjury, burn incense to Baal and follow other gods you have not known, and then come and stand before me in this house, which bears my Name, and say, 'We are safe'—safe to do all these detestable things? Has this house, which bears my Name, become a den of robbers to you? But I have been watching! declares the LORD."

In context, Jeremiah is speaking to people who use worship as a shelter for their immorality. He likens them to thieves who steal and then sneak off to a hideout to count up the spoils. He says that in doing so, they are turning God's house into a "den of robbers." Jesus views the Temple as the place where the robbers count the spoils of the immorality of their everyday lives.

Fruit, Not Leaves

Discipleship is about following Jesus, the one who was tempted in every way as we are, yet was without sin. We are to be perfect as our heavenly Father is perfect. This perfection that we seek through discipleship isn't primarily ritual but, rather, ethical. As God says through the prophet Hosea, "I desire mercy, not sacrifice" (Hos 6:6). We might say in light of these two stories in Mark 11 that **God desires fruit, not leaves**. God desires more than the appearance of fruitfulness, he desires fruitfulness.

> God desires fruit, not leaves.

At their core, both the Temple cleansing and the cursing of the fig tree are about the same thing—being faithful all of the time. Not only in season, but out of season as well. Not only in the Temple, but out of the Temple. Not only in the church building, but between Sundays as well.

Just as a fruit tree is useless out of season, so is faith that turns on and off with the times. Our fruit is to be borne at all times—between Sundays, each minute of each day. Disciples bear fruit in all seasons. Not only when things are going our way. Not only when it benefits us directly. We bear fruit even when we don't feel like bearing fruit. This is real discipleship. This is God's will for us in Christ. The good news is that God has not left us alone to struggle with the task of constant fruit-bearing. He has given us the Holy Spirit as his power and presence to transform us into the likeness of Christ. As Paul says: "But the fruit of the Spirit is love, joy, peace, patience, kindness, goodness, faithfulness, gentleness and self-control. Against such things there is no law. Those who belong to Christ Jesus have crucified the sinful nature with its passions and desires. Since we live by the Spirit, let us keep in step with the Spirit" (Gal 5:22-25).

What happens in the cleansing of the Temple is the same thing that happens in the cursing of the fig tree. **Jesus outwardly rebukes seasonal fruitbearing.** The fig tree has beautiful leaves but bears no fruit. In a sense the Temple and all it represents is the same as the barren fig tree. In a season when the kingdom of God has come near, the Temple is a place where those who should be able to eat its fruits go away hungry because it has been turned into "a den of robbers." Just as those who look to the fig tree for fruit go away hungry and disappointed, so those who go to the Temple for worship find not a house of prayer for all nations, but a den of robbers.

The Fruitful Church

On September 6, 1520, Martin Luther penned an open letter to Pope Leo X. He wrote: "The Roman church, once the holiest of all, has become the most licentious den of thieves, the most shameless of all brothels, the kingdom of sin, death, and hell. It is so bad that even the Antichrist himself, if he should come, could think of nothing to add to its wickedness." Luther's words may seem harsh to us, but words calling God's people back toward faithfulness have always played a vital role in helping God's people stay focused on the cross. Luther was saying in his time that the church was becoming a den of robbers.

In our time, we should never consent to become a den of robbers— a place where we all take shelter and appear faithful after living worship-free lives between Sundays. Worship is where the sinners-made-saints of God gather to boldly proclaim his Lordship with one voice. When we leave, we do the same through how we live.

These two stories in Mark 11 are a word of exhortation to us. Let us listen. The word is not that if we sin we will be cursed. God's grace is far too deep and wide for that. However, people or churches that over time become dens of robbers *are* cursed, their tables are turned over, or to put it in the words of Jesus in the book of Revelation, their lampstands are taken away (cf. Rev 2:4-5).

This is a word of God to us. A difficult word to be sure, but a word of God nonetheless. Let us then delight in it and meditate upon it day and night that we might become "like trees planted by streams of water who bear their fruit in season and out of season, whose leaves do not wither and who prosper in all they do" (Ps 1:3, paraphrase).

---

[1]Joseph Klausner, *Jesus of Nazareth* (London: George Allen and Unwin, 1925) 269.
[2]Cited by C.E.B. Cranfield, *The Gospel according to St. Mark*, Cambridge Greek Testament Commentary (Cambridge: Cambridge University Press, 1966) 356.

83

‡

C
H
A
P
T
E
R

Cleansing the Temple 11

Servants Like Jesus

1. What is Mark's "Sandwich Technique?"

2. Are you shocked by Jesus' anger in these stories?

3. Think about a time when you felt a sense of "righteous indignation."

4. The author claims that "God desires fruit, not leaves." What does he mean?

5. Name some "leaves" that people display to look spiritual and cover up fruitlessness.

6. Why is it hard to be honest with others about our spiritual barrenness?

| **Memory Verse** Mark 11:24-25 | *Therefore I tell you, whatever you ask for in prayer, believe that you have received it, and it will be yours. And when you stand praying, if you hold anything against anyone, forgive him, so that your Father in heaven may forgive you your sins.* |

CHAPTER TWELVE

BECOMING A "CROSSTIAN"

MARK 15:25-34

It was the third hour when they crucified him. The written notice of the charge against him read: THE KING OF THE JEWS. They crucified two robbers with him, one on his right and one on his left. Those who passed by hurled insults at him, shaking their heads and saying, "So! You who are going to destroy the temple and build it in three days, come down from the cross and save yourself!" In the same way the chief priests and the teachers of the law mocked him among themselves. "He saved others," they said, "but he can't save himself! Let this Christ, this King of Israel, come down now from the cross, that we may see and believe." Those crucified with him also heaped insults on him. At the sixth hour darkness came over the whole land until the ninth hour. And at the ninth hour Jesus cried out in a loud voice, *"Eloi, Eloi, lama sabachthani?"*—which means, "My God, my God, why have you forsaken me?" (Mark 15:25-34).

Anyone who examines Christianity for the first time will notice the extraordinary amount of stress that Jesus' followers put on his death. In every other religion, a leader's death is lamented as the end of an illustrious career. What matters in most religions is the life and teaching of the leader. Death itself is of little importance. For Christianity, it is the other way around. To be sure, Jesus life and teachings were incomparable. Yet, from the beginning, Christians have taught everyone seeking Christ how immensely important his death is.

When the Gospels came to be written, Matthew, Mark, Luke, and John devoted a disproportionate amount of space to the last week of Jesus' life on earth—in the case of Luke a quarter, of Matthew and Mark about a third, and of John as much as a half. When they wrote these biographies of Christ under the inspiration of God's Spirit, they focused intently on his death.

It is also clear that Jesus' death was central to his self-understanding. Mark tells us of three occasions on which Jesus predicted his death, saying that, "the Son of Man must suffer many things . . . and . . . be killed" (Mark 8:31; cf. 9:31; 10:32-34). In the mind of Christ, his death on the cross was the fulfillment of his mission. It had to take place. He referred to it as "the hour" for which he had come into the world.

On the night before his death, Jesus even made provision for his own memorial service. He asked the apostles to take bread and remember his body, broken for them. Then he asked them to drink wine in memory of his blood poured out for them. Both images—the breaking of bread and the pouring out of wine, speak of death. At the Last Supper, Jesus let his followers know how he wished to be remembered, and for what. Jesus wanted us to remember his death.

The church then has been right to choose the cross as its symbol for Christianity. John Stott has pointed out that the church could have chosen the crib as a symbol of incarnation or the carpenter's bench as a way of affirming the dignity of manual labor. The church could have chosen a boat from where Jesus taught the people or a towel with which he demonstrated servanthood by washing the disciples' feet. The church could have the tomb from which he rose or the dove or fire. Any of these are appropriate symbols of the Christian faith. Yet, the church passed all of them by in favor of the cross, which stands for the necessity and centrality of Jesus' death.[1]

The choice of the cross as the supreme Christian symbol is all the more remarkable because in Greco-Roman society the cross was a symbol of shame. The cross was reserved by the Romans for their worst criminals and their most dastardly traitors. No Roman citizen was ever crucified. Cicero condemned crucifixion as *"a most cruel and disgusting punishment."*[2] And in his famous defense of an elderly senator he insisted that *"the very word 'cross' should be far removed not only from the person of a Roman citizen, but from his thoughts, his eyes and his ears."*[3]

> Jesus' death sets him apart from other religious leaders of history.

Jesus' death sets him apart from other religious leaders of history. Most died in a good old age, having successfully completed their mission. Muhammad was 62, Confucius 72, the Buddha 80, and Moses 120. But Jesus died the horrible death of crucifixion in his early thirties, rejected by his own people, apparently a complete and utter failure—yet claiming that by his death he was fulfilling his mission.

Because He Loved Us So

Jesus died, because he wanted to, out of his love for people. Some people have portrayed Jesus as one convicted against his will and put to death by sinners against his will. It is true that Jesus was crucified by sinners. However, we must always remember that *Jesus died according to, not against, God's will* because of his love for all people. Jesus died willingly, because he loves us. He explains in John 10:11,18: "I am the good shepherd. The good shepherd lays down his life for the sheep. No one takes it from me, but I lay it down of my own accord. I have authority to lay it down and authority to take it up again. This command I received from my Father."

I will be the first to admit that this doesn't really make sense. Why would someone give their life for the sins of others? How could Jesus actually want to die even for the sins of those who crucified him?

I don't get it. I don't get it because I love my life more than I love my neighbor. I don't get it because I have a tough time loving those who don't love me. I don't get it because Christ's love is superior to my own, and for that I am thankful.

Toward Crosstianity

The cross calls me not just to receive its benefits but to receive it as a way of life. The cross is more than a monument or a symbol for Christianity. The cross is the daily mission of the Christian church. Jesus died to give us something to imitate. In Luke 14:27, Jesus says, "And anyone who does not carry his cross and follow me cannot be my disciple."

The cross is a beautiful yet gloriously difficult reality which shows us what life lived radically for God can do to you. Taking up the way of the kingdom means we will bear the brunt of the sin and fear of a yet unredeemed world.

I wonder if we too often miss what may be the most powerful impact the cross should have on our lives. When speaking of the cross's implications, we often use language like, "Jesus died so you don't have to," or "He did this for you." I understand what we mean by this and there is great truth to these statements. Jesus did die to redeem us from our sins. However, the cross is more than atonement for our sins. The cross is both where Jesus dies in our place *and* where he invites us to die with him. In the cross, he invites us to joyfully accept suffering and joyfully bear

> The cross is both where Jesus dies in our place and where he invites us to die with him.

the injustices and the oppression and rebellion of our world. This is the present and coming kingdom of God.

This is a strange message for those of us living in 21st-century America because we don't do pain if it can be avoided. We are far and away the most prescribed culture in the world—that is, we take more drugs than any other country in the world to avoid feeling any pain. We will do just about anything to escape pain: take drugs (illegal or pre-scribed), alcohol, or anything else that will get rid of the pain.

I was watching TV one night and I had a bit of a headache. Just then, a commercial came on. A dad was smiling and throwing his little girl in the air and catching her again as they laughed. You may have seen it. I don't even know what the drug was for. The commercial just said, "Ask your doctor if (such and such drug) is right for you." (Throw and catch). After 30 seconds of watching Dad catch his daughter, a very soothing voice came on in the background: "Side effects may include nausea, blurred vision, brain damage, stomach pains, itchy skin, dementia, and in some cases, death." No thanks, I thought, I'll take the headache. Even taking pain-relieving drugs is too painful for us these days!

Nevertheless, when Jesus describes the Christian life, he still has the gall to use words like "cross," "sacrifice," "lay down your life." Does God really think he is going to get anywhere with that kind of message?

It is precisely in times like these that the message of the cross is most breathtaking and profound. It is in times like these that Christians must renew their commitment to a faith founded on the *death* of their leader. If we don't, our insistence on pain-free living will impact virtu-ally every area of our lives. It will impact our witness because our desire to avoid any suffering will keep us from speaking truth when we need to. It will impact our integrity as our desire to escape the consequences of our mistakes leads us to lie and cheat. It will impact our children as we model soft faith before them day in and day out. May it never be that our kids struggle with humility and service when they are grown because we never modeled these things for them and never asked them to give up something for the sake of someone else. To go a step further, a lack of cross in Christianity will impact the work of the church as our desire to avoid suffering keeps us from giving the way we should or from serving in ways that cost us something.

Thomas à Kempis was right when he said: "Jesus now has many lovers of his heavenly kingdom, but few bearers of his cross." There are indeed many counterfeit versions of Christianity which teach that the cross was for Jesus only, and that our job is to sit back and enjoy all of the benefits it brings without the claims it makes on our lives. We should rejoice in the grace of the cross, but we should allow that grace to lead us toward cruciform lives, as well.

The cross of Christ stands before us, calling us to do without for the sake of others and to endure suffering for the sake of his name. The cross calls us to sacrifice our resources for the sake of the kingdom and to care about those who don't care about us. The cross calls us to pray for our enemies and to do all types of things that won't gratify our appetites. When it's all said and done, the cross is still the core of who we are. When we forget that, we have lost it all.

To be Christian is to be a "Crosstian." To be a disciple means the willingness to pick up our cross and follow him. We shouldn't be afraid of the cross. We should rush to pick it up and carry it in the steps of Jesus Christ—the one who picked up his cross for us.

Some believe that it is never God's will that they should suffer. The Bible tells us though that suffering is often a sign that we are living a Christlike life:

> If you endure when you are beaten for doing wrong, what credit is that? But if you endure when you do right and suffer for it, you have God's approval. For to this you have been called, because Christ also suffered for you, leaving you an example, so that you should follow in his steps. "He committed no sin, and no deceit was found in his mouth." When he was abused, he did not return abuse; when he suffered, he did not threaten; but he entrusted himself to the one who judges justly. He himself bore our sins in his body on the cross, so that, free from sins, we might live for righteousness; by his wounds you have been healed (1 Pet 2:20-24).

Because of their faith, some people have stopped the mouths of lions, have won wars, have raised the dead, and have had every kind of triumph you can imagine. And yet, there have been others who have ended up *in* the mouths of lions, or a little poorer, or with one less vacation house, or without the fame they once so desired. Faith is sometimes a success story, and sometimes not. It is always a story that says, "I take up my cross and follow Jesus, come what may."

Why am I a Christian?

Why am I a Christian? Because the same cross that is my salvation is also my daily call to worship. I am a Christian because the one I love, Jesus Christ, laid his life down for me and has asked me to do the same. His promise is that if I will lose my life, I will save it. If I try to save my life, I will lose it. Jesus has shown us how to live, how to die, and how to rise. Paul tells us:

Let the same mind be in you that was in Christ Jesus, who, though he was in the form of God, did not regard equality with God as something to be exploited, but emptied himself, taking the form of a slave, being born in human likeness. And being found in human form, he humbled himself and became obedient to the point of death—even death on a cross. Therefore God also highly exalted him and gave him the name that is above every name, so that at the name of Jesus every knee should bend, in heaven and on earth and under the earth, and every tongue should confess that Jesus Christ is Lord, to the glory of God the Father (Phil 2:5-11).

Let all who agree say, "Amen," and pick up their crosses together to follow Christ. [2:16]

[1]John R.W. Stott, *Why I Am a Christian* (Downers Grove, IL: InterVarsity, 2003) 51.
[2]Cicero, *Against Veres* 2.64.165.
[3]Cicero, *In Defense of Rabirius* 5.16.467.

12 *Becoming a "Crosstian"*

Servants Like Jesus

1. What makes Jesus' death different from the death of other religious leaders?

2. Why do we flee pain as much as we do? What impact do you think that has on our faith?

3. What teachings of Jesus, if taken seriously, would potentially bring the most suffering into your life?

4. In what ways have you avoided suffering for Jesus' sake?

5. The author states, ". . . the same cross that is my salvation is also my daily call to worship." What does he mean by this?

6. Have you accepted Jesus' invitation to the cross? If not, why not?

Memory Verse Mark 15:37-39	*With a loud cry, Jesus breathed his last. The curtain of the temple was torn in two from top to bottom. And when the centurion, who stood there in front of Jesus, heard his cry and saw how he died, he said, "Surely this man was the Son of God!"*

CHAPTER THIRTEEN

GO AND TELL

MARK 16:1-8,14-18

My wife Emily and I used to live in a small town in northern California. Out where the church building was located, the town was even smaller. There were very few stoplights along long, narrow, winding roads. At night headlights meant nothing. It was just plain dark. Every now and then there would be an accident on one of the roads. You could see the ambulance lights for miles because of the darkness.

No matter where I go, people always slow down when they get to the scene of an accident. It isn't because people simply enjoy tragedy. People slow down to look because of what accidents make them think about. When a person views the scene of an accident, they think, "That could have been me." Then we might wonder . . . "Who was it?" "Why them?" "Why not me?" "Why not someone else?" "Could something have prevented this?"

These are the types of questions going through the minds of Jesus' followers as Mark 16 opens three days after the wreckage of the cross. Disillusioned and unaware of what is about to happen, Mary and her friends head to the graveyard seeking to honor the body of Jesus by anointing him with spices. As they do, the questions continue.

> And they asked each other, "Who will roll the stone away from the entrance of the tomb?" But when they looked up, they saw that the stone, which was very large, had been rolled away. As they entered the tomb, they saw a young man dressed in a white robe sitting on the

right side, and they were alarmed. "Don't be alarmed," he said. "You are looking for Jesus the Nazarene, who was crucified. He has risen! He is not here. See the place where they laid him. But go, tell his disciples and Peter, 'He is going ahead of you into Galilee. There you will see him, just as he told you.'" Trembling and bewildered, the women went out and fled from the tomb. They said nothing to anyone, because they were afraid (Mark 16:3-8).

What a moment! Of all the things that he had ever done, this topped it all. Victory was his, even over death! He was Lord after all! Not even death could hold him!

The normal reaction (or so we think) to such wonders is praise and amazement. However, Mark tells us Mary, Mary, and Salome have a different response. They are terrified. What should amaze them terrifies them. God's work often does this because our humanness limits our ability to see what God is up to. Other times his power is so awesome it actually scares us.

We humans don't always recognize God's work as such at first sight. Nowhere is this more obvious than in the work of God through Christ. Listen to how the Apostle John put it: "But although the world was made through him, the world didn't recognize him when he came" (John 1:10). Throughout Mark's Gospel, those who should recognize Jesus as God's Chosen One don't; those who shouldn't do. At the empty tomb, Mary, Mary, and Salome should have been expecting an empty tomb. Instead, the empty tomb leaves them "trembling and bewildered."

> We humans don't always recognize God's work as such at first sight.

Teaching Resurrection

There has been a tremendous emphasis in recent years upon the earthly life and ministry of Jesus. Scholars have studied "the historical Jesus." Christians, for good reason, have studied the human characteristics of Jesus in order to follow him more deeply. This is all fine and good, but we must never lose sight of the fact that Jesus is God's Son, and that through him all things were created, he is Lord of all, and that he was raised. Preaching a "personal Jesus" that doesn't help people understand Jesus as God is harmful in the long run.

Mark goes out of his way to help us see that Jesus can do *anything*—even though his followers have a hard time believing it. The scene at the empty tomb is another case in point. We must make sure that we spend plenty of time at the empty tomb's entrance. The resurrection is the core of what we believe. It is at the core of Jesus' divinity. Luke Timothy Johnson said, ". . . if the resurrection is excluded, why should Christians continue to revere Jesus, who is then only one of many figures from antiquity worthy of attention and honor? If Jesus is only the 'historical Jesus,' then Christianity is a delusion and a waste of time. But, if Jesus Christ is raised as Lord, everything changes radically."[1]

Christ is alive. We accept this by faith and allow it to transform us. God keeps his promises. Nowhere is this more the case than as it pertains to the resurrection. Scripture points to several realities that fill us with confidence that Jesus has indeed raised. As we teach and learn more about the resurrection, we rely on faith. The following truths further bolster our faith in what God did at the empty tomb:

1. Jesus predicted his resurrection (Matt 16:21; Mark 9:9-10; John 2:18-22).
2. The Old Testament prophesied it (Ps 16:10; compare Acts 2:25-31; 13:33-37).
3. The tomb was empty and the grave clothes vacant. If those who opposed Christ wished to silence his disciples, all they had to do was produce a body, but they could not (John 20:3-9).
4. Many people saw the resurrected Christ. They looked on his face, touched him, heard his voice, and saw him eat (Matt 28:16-20; Luke 24:13-39; John 20:11-29; 21:1-9; Acts 1:6-11; 1 Cor 15:3-8).
5. The lives of the disciples were revolutionized. Though they fled and even denied Christ at the time of his arrest, they later feared no one in their proclamation of the risen Christ (Matt 26:56,69-75).
6. The resurrection was the central message of the early church. The church grew with an unwavering conviction that Christ had risen and was the Lord of the church (Acts 4:33; 5:30-32; Rom 5:24).
7. Men and women today testify that the power of the risen Christ has transformed their lives. We know that Jesus is alive not only because of the historical and biblical evidence but also because he has miraculously touched our lives and grown our faith.

I have not seen anyone physically dead get up again. Nevertheless, I believe that Jesus did so. Why? Because others saw him, and because I have seen him. I see his miracles still taking place. I see death being turned to life all around me. I see lives being changed all around me. And I have hope because Christ died and was raised by the power of God.

The resurrection of Jesus is more than the resuscitation of a human being. Jesus' resurrection was a once-and-for-all resurrection. His resurrection broke the back of death. This separates him from all other religious leaders. He *alone* is the resurrection and the life.

. . . it has been said:

- Other religious leaders tell people, "Follow me and I'll show you how to find truth," but Jesus says, "I am the truth."
- Other religious leaders tell people, "Follow me and I'll show you the way to salvation," but Jesus says, "I am the way to eternal life."
- Other religious leaders tell people, "Follow me and I'll show you how to become enlightened," but Jesus says, "I am the light of the world."
- Other religious leaders tell people, "Follow me and I'll show you many doors that lead to God," but Jesus says, "I am the door." Then Jesus says, "So follow me."

Do you see the difference?[2]

Our Resurrection

The Bible proclaims boldly and repeatedly that Christ rose on the third day and is now seated at the right hand of God. Scripture also teaches that just as Christ was raised, we too will be raised!

The resurrection of Jesus is the foundation of our hope for a better day—a day when there will be no pain, grief, or sorrow—a day when every tear will be dry and we will surround the throne and worship our Lord forever. Paul says in 1 Corinthians15:14 that if the resurrection isn't true then our faith is worthless. Thus, the resurrection changes everything. It changes how we live and how we die.

Resurrection Points Us toward Mission

As Mark comes to a close, Jesus leaves his disciples with these words:

He said to them, "Go into all the world and preach the good news to all creation. Whoever believes and is baptized will be saved, but whoever does not believe will be condemned. And these signs will accompany those who believe: In my name they will drive out demons; they will speak in new tongues; they will pick up snakes with their hands; and when they drink deadly poison, it will not hurt them at all; they will place their hands on sick people, and they will get well" (Mark 16:15-18).

The resurrection calls us to mission because we serve a risen Lord who is still preaching, moving, and working. When he comes again, we too will be raised to live with him forever. Those who do not believe "will be condemned." God will give us strength to preach the gospel more fervently than ever. *We must.*

Prevailing culture isn't helping anymore. The government isn't helping anymore. The media isn't helping anymore. The schools aren't helping anymore. **That's okay, because we are supposed to be the ones speaking the good news.** *It has always been the charge of the church to proclaim the truth about Jesus, whether or not the culture supports it.*

> It has always been the charge of the church to proclaim the truth about Jesus, whether or not the culture supports it.

Christianity is not fundamentally a civic faith. It was born through crucifixion, persecution, and minority status within culture. It is in such circumstances that Christianity has proven to be most vibrant. Society's margins form a wonderful pulpit from which to share Christ.

This is good news for us living in America today. It is in times like these that we must stand up and boldly proclaim that Jesus Christ is Lord and the only way to God. *There is no other way.* Jesus is the first and the last, the Son of God, the full atonement for our sins, the everlasting God, the lover of our souls, the way, the truth, the life. No one comes to the Father except through Jesus, the Raised One.

Before we preach, however, let's read the warning label. If you preach the gospel, you will be persecuted. You may be called narrow-minded, a fundamentalist, or a heretic. Preach anyway.

If Christians are unwilling to stand up and proclaim the gospel boldly they have lost their witness and taken their rightful place among the other mundane and impotent so-called religions of the world. If, on

> Before we preach, let's read the warning label.

the other hand, God's people share their faith with passion and unswerving boldness, lives will change. The world will change because Christ will be lifted up.

We now continue the ministry of the Raised One. We are the community of the raised. Because he was raised and we will be raised, we stand up and proclaim boldly the gospel of Jesus Christ. Our voice, though dissonant with the surrounding culture, must be heard. The following challenge was issued in a church newsletter:

Jesus.
It's a little name.
A small word.
Say this little name in public, however, in a way other than an obscenity, and stand back and watch the fireworks.
This little name is like a tiny detonator that triggers a nuclear warhead.

You can say "God," and you won't get a squeak.
You can say "Our Father/Mother in Heaven," and few will flinch.
You can say "Great Spirit," and people will nod in approval.
You can say "Allah," and you will be deemed tolerant.
But say "Jesus," and just wait for the sonic boom.
Articles will appear in the paper.
Reprimands will be posted from the home office.
Suits will be threatened by the civil liberties block.
So don't say Jesus.
Jesus is divisive, and now is a time for unity.
Jesus is an extremist, and that must mean right wing.
Jesus is exclusive, so his name amounts to hate speech.
Keep his name to yourself. Cloister it in your church. Lock it in your
prayer closet. Close it between the covers of your Bible.
But for God's sake, don't voice it in the public square!
It's immodest. It's immoral. It's unloving.
Only one problem.
Jesus is God.
Only one problem.
Jesus alone brings salvation.
Only one problem.
All other gods are nothing.
So speak his name aloud.
Shout it from the mountain.
Whisper it in the dark.
Write it in the sky.
That's not hate, it's hope."[3]

In John 11:25-26, Jesus says: "I am the resurrection and the life. He who believes in me will live, even though he dies; and whoever lives and believes in me will never die."

This is soul food for all who would come after Jesus. He is the resurrection and life. All who believe in him will live even in death. All who follow Jesus will never die. If we believe this, these words of Jesus, all of their promises are ours. Hallelujah! ▣

---

[1]Luke Timothy Johnson, *The Creed* (New York: Doubleday, 2003) 180.
[2]Lee Strobel, *God's Outrageous Claims: Discover What They Mean for You* (Grand Rapids: Zondervan, 2005).
[3]Southeast Christian Church Newsletter, Louisville, KY. Original date of publication unknown. Cited frequently in sermons due to its inclusion in a study guide for *The Passion of the Christ*.

Servants Like Jesus

1. Describe a time when God's actions terrified you.

2. Describe how you would have felt at the empty tomb if you had been there with Mary, Mary, and Salome.

3. Why is Jesus' resurrection so central to the Christian faith?

4. In what circumstances is it most difficult to share your faith?

5. Is Christianity more "effective" in cultures that are friendlier to the gospel or in cultures that appear to be less friendly toward the gospel?

6. What will heaven be like? Describe it as you picture it.

Memory Verse
Mark 16:15-16

He said to them, "Go into all the world and preach the good news to all creation. Whoever believes and is baptized will be saved, but whoever does not believe will be condemned."

About the Author

Tim Spivey has served as the Senior Minister for the Highland Oaks Church of Christ in Dallas, Texas, since October of 2002. With a heart and passion for God that is contagious, Tim is a gifted preacher who communicates God's Word in ways that are insightful, challenging, and relevant. Tim is perhaps best known for drawing applications out of difficult texts and presenting them in an engaging way.

Tim and his wife Emily are parents of two girls, Anna and Olivia. Prior to serving in Dallas, Tim served as a youth minister, campus minister, worship minister, and preaching minister for churches in California and Texas. He holds a Bachelor of Arts degree in Religion, a Masters of Science degree in Ministry, and a Masters of Divinity degree from Pepperdine University. He is currently pursuing a Doctor of Ministry degree from Abilene Christian University.

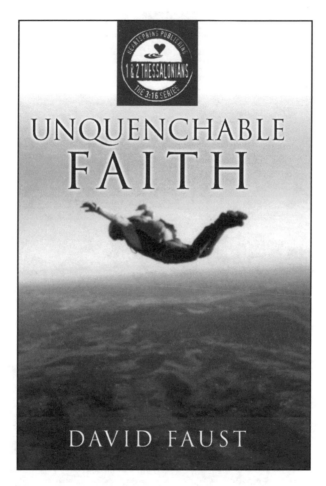

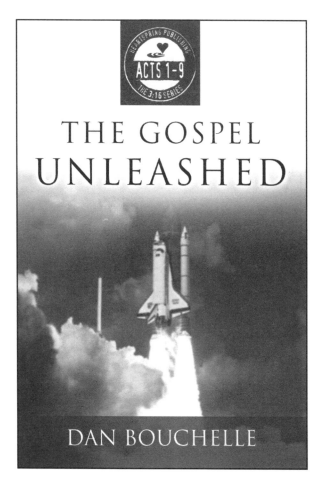

The Gospel Unleashed
Acts 1-9

Dan Bouchelle

137 pages, softbound, 316M-493-8, $6.99

1-800-289-3300 • www.collegepress.com

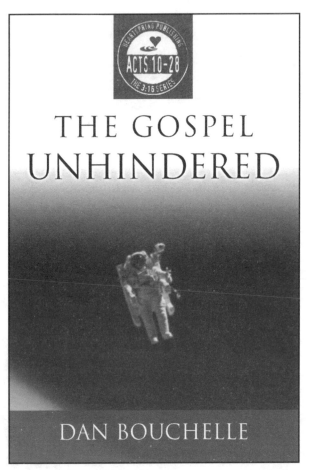

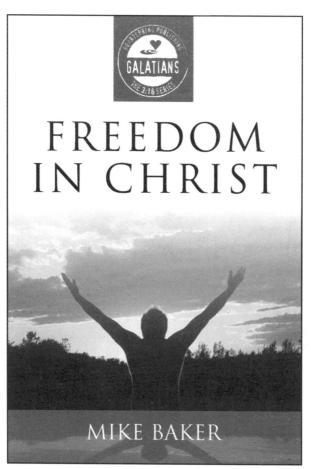

Freedom in Christ
Galatians
Mike Baker

112 pages, softbound, 316M-299-4, $6.99

1-800-289-3300 • www.collegepress.com

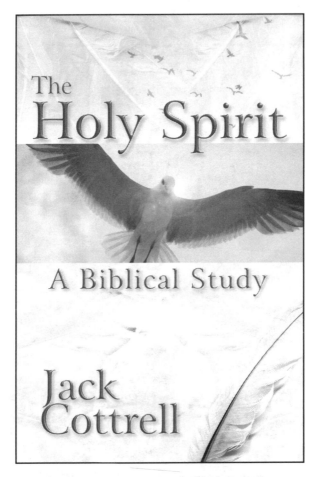

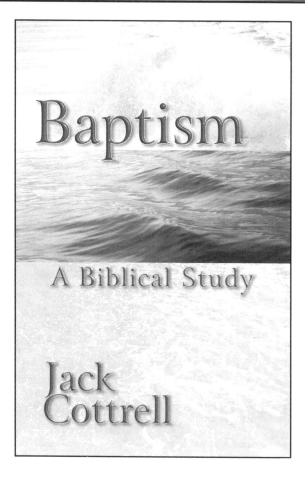

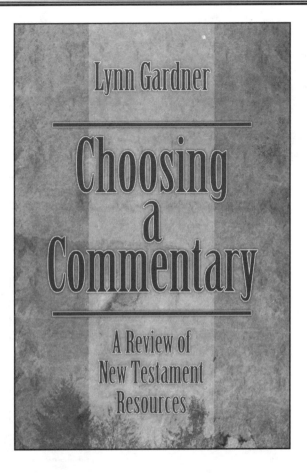

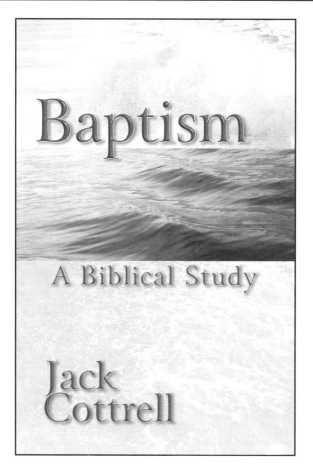

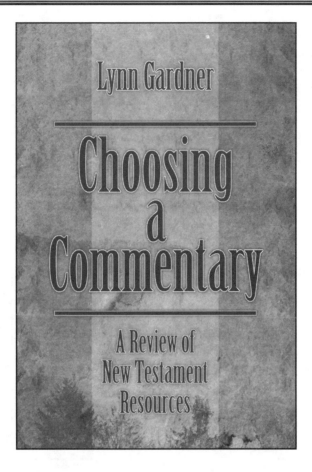

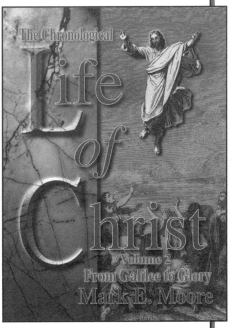

MARK MEMORY VERSES

HEART SPRING

✂ Cut on dotted line

Mark 1:27 (NIV)
27 The people were all so amazed that they asked each other, "What is this? A new teaching—and with authority! He even gives orders to evil spirits and they obey him."

Mark 2:27-28 (NIV)
27 Then he said to them, "The Sabbath was made for man, not man for the Sabbath. 28 So the Son of Man is Lord even of the Sabbath."

Mark 3: 34-35 (NIV)
34 Then he looked at those seated in a circle around him and said, "Here are my mother and my brothers! 35 Whoever does God's will is my brother and sister and mother."

Mark 4:30-32 (NIV)
30 Again he said, "What shall we say the kingdom of God is like, or what parable shall we use to describe it? 31 It is like a mustard seed, which is the smallest seed you plant in the ground. 32 Yet when planted, it grows and becomes the largest of all garden plants, with such big branches that the birds of the air can perch in its shade."

Philippians 4:6-7 (NIV)
6 Do not be anxious about anything, but in everything, by prayer and petition, with thanksgiving, present your requests to God. 7 And the peace of God, which transcends all understanding, will guard your hearts and your minds in Christ Jesus.

Mark 5:35-36 (NIV)
35 While Jesus was still speaking, some men came from the house of Jairus, the synagogue ruler. "Your daughter is dead," they said. "Why bother the teacher any more?" 36 Ignoring what they said, Jesus told the synagogue ruler, "Don't be afraid; just believe."

Mark 8:34-35 (NIV)
34 Then he called the crowd to him along with his disciples and said: "If anyone would come after me, he must deny himself and take up his cross and follow me. 35 For whoever wants to save his life will lose it, but whoever loses his life for me and for the gospel will save it.

Mark 9:7-8 (NIV)
7 Then a cloud appeared and enveloped them, and a voice came from the cloud: "This is my Son, whom I love. Listen to him!"
8 Suddenly, when they looked around, they no longer saw anyone with them except Jesus.

Mark 9:28-29 (NIV)
28 After Jesus had gone indoors, his disciples asked him privately, "Why couldn't we drive it out?" 29 He replied, "This kind can come out only by prayer. "

Mark 9:38-40 (NIV)
38 "Teacher," said John, "we saw a man driving out demons in your name and we told him to stop, because he was not one of us." 39 "Do not stop him," Jesus said. "No one who does a miracle in my name can in the next moment say anything bad about me, 40 for whoever is not against us is for us.

Mark 11:24-25 (NIV)
24 Therefore I tell you, whatever you ask for in prayer, believe that you have received it, and it will be yours. 25 And when you stand praying, if you hold anything against anyone, forgive him, so that your Father in heaven may forgive you your sins. "

Mark 15:37-39 (NIV)
37 With a loud cry, Jesus breathed his last. 38 The curtain of the temple was torn in two from top to bottom. 39 And when the centurion, who stood there in front of Jesus, heard his cry and saw how he died, he said, "Surely this man was the Son of God!"

Mark 16:15-16 (NIV)
15 He said to them, "Go into all the world and preach the good news to all creation. 16 Whoever believes and is baptized will be saved, but whoever does not believe will be condemned.